UNCLASSIFIED

AD NUMBER

AD074148

NEW LIMITATION CHANGE

TO

Approved for public release, distribution unlimited

FROM

Distribution authorized to U.S. Gov't. agencies and their contractors; Administrative/Operational Use; DEC 1952. Other requests shall be referred to Air University, Human Resources Research Inst., Maxwell AFB. AL.

AUTHORITY

19 mar 2008 per AF AU ltr

THIS PAGE IS UNCLASSIFIED

74148

Services Technical Information Agency

Guide to
CAPTURED GERMAN DOCUMENTS

Air University

Human Resources Research Institute

Maxwell Air Force Base, Alabama

December 1952

Research Memorandum
NUMBER 2
Vol. 1

HRRI
"War Documentation Project"

WAR DOCUMENTATION PROJECT
STUDY NO. 1:

Guide to Captured German Documents

Prepared by

GERHARD L. WEINBERG

and

the WDP staff

under the direction of

FRITZ T. EPSTEIN

Prepared under contract AF 18 (600-1) with
THE BUREAU OF APPLIED SOCIAL RESEARCH
COLUMBIA UNIVERSITY

UNITED STATES AIR FORCE
AIR UNIVERSITY
HUMAN RESOURCES RESEARCH INSTITUTE
Maxwell Air Force Base, Alabama

1 September 1952

The War Documentation Project (WDP) is being conducted
under Air Force contract by the Bureau of Applied Social
Research, Columbia University. It is a major research activity of the Psychological Warfare Directorate of this
Institute. Mr. Hans J. Epstein serves as Project Officer.

The War Documentation Project was conceived to answer
a long-standing requirement for the systematic research ex-
ploitation of the vast masses of captured documents which
came into the hands of the United States Government during
and after World War II. The project was planned in two
phases. Under Phase I the significant depositories of such
documents were to be located and their contents surveyed and
catalogued. Under Phase II the documentary holdings thus
surveyed are to be exploited for systematic research, focus-
ing on tasks in the psychological warfare and intelligence
fields. Phase I was undertaken with the aid and support of
the Department of the Army, the Department of the Navy, and
the Department of State. This phase was completed in June
1952, and Phase II was initiated soon afterwards.

The present volume is to be regarded as a by-product of
Phase I. The collection and publication of this guide was
not originally contemplated or called for in the contract,
but as the work of the WDP staff progressed towards its pre-
scribed goal, the information here assembled was accu-
rulated.

For a long time scholars and researchers have been con-
tributing to the efforts of the Armed Forces of our country.
In doing so, their professional identity has been sacrificed
to the anonymity demanded by security restriction. It is
with very real satisfaction, therefore, that the United
States Air Force makes available a volume which primarily
meets scholarly needs, although it results from a governmental research undertaking of restricted scope and opera-
tionally defined focus.

I feel certain that the Guide to Captured German Documents
will be but the first in a significant and useful series of
publications produced by the War Documentation Project.

F. O. CARROLL
Major General, USAF
Commandant

Preface

THIS *Guide* to captured German documents is the out-growth of efforts on the part of the War Documentation Project (WDP) to secure as accurate information as possible on the fate and location of freely accessible German documentary sources scattered by the fate of war. It should be noted that the term "captured documents" is used here not with its limited legal significance; the expression is applied, in a generalizing and abbreviating sense, to German materials which through capture, confiscation, purchase, donation, salvage, etc., were transferred to non-German control during or after World War II.

As more and more information on German documentary holdings outside Germany accumulated, it seemed useful to make a compilation of the data gathered generally available. The difficulties encountered in collecting this information for the War Documentation Project itself—difficulties which have presumably confronted other organizations and individuals—greatly strengthened the intention of publishing this *Guide*.

The *Guide* has been prepared on a co-operative basis; several members of the staff of the WDP have made important contributions. The following staff members aided in collecting the information: Kurt DeWitt, Wilhelm Moll, Frances Mond, Hans Weil, and Earl Ziemke.

Philip E. Mosely, Director of the Russian Institute, Columbia University, and Senior Consultant to the WDP, has been the principal advisor to the project since its inception; to his unflagging efforts and endeavors the WDP in general, and this, its first publication, in particular, owes a singular debt of gratitude. The task of putting some form into the material has benefited from the labors of exceedingly patient and devoted secretaries, Mrs. Jean S. Powell and Mrs. Margot W. Moll.

The bibliography owes much to the generous aid received from the administrations and staffs of several institutions. The cooperation of the Library of Congress; the National Archives; the Hoover Institute and Library; the Yiddish Scientific Institute (YIVO); the Centre de Documentation Juive Contemporaine; République Française, Présidence du Conseil, Comité d'Histoire de la Guerre; and the Netherlands State Institute for War-Documentation is gratefully acknowledged.

The willingness of the Air University to offer its publishing facilities for the printing of the *Guide* as *War Documentation Project, (Research Memorandum Number 2, Vol. 1)* has encouraged its preparation and is greatly appreciated.

Alexandria, Virginia
May 31, 1952.

FRITZ T. EPSTEIN
Principal Investigator
War Documentation Project

v

Table of Contents

General Introduction

At the end of World War II, documents of German Government agencies, military organizations, and political and private groups were scattered or destroyed in large numbers. No comprehensive survey of the surviving records and their location is available. No such survey is likely to become available for a long period of time. Little is known about the considerable quantity of German records which fell into the hands of Germany's eastern enemies; and probably a far greater quantity of documents is presently kept in various classified collections of Western Powers. The great importance of the German documents for research purposes, however, makes it very desirable that a preliminary survey, at least of the unrestricted German materials to be found in certain American, Dutch, English, and French depositories, be made accessible to government agencies and private scholars.

The War Documentation Project has attempted to bring together printed as well as hitherto unpublished information on captured, non-technical German documents. Therefore, on the one hand, an effort has been made to compile listings of books and periodicals containing either the text of captured German documents, citations of such documents in footnotes, or information concerning the location of document holdings (Parts I and II). On the other hand, the War Documentation Project has prepared or secured detailed listings of the German documents in the most important depositories, particularly the Library of Congress (Part III).

In all the listings, materials used in the war crimes and collaborationist trials have been omitted. Furthermore, only holdings of unclassified depositories* are listed. This means that all documents mentioned in Part III on depositories are accessible to the general public, subject only to the internal regulations of the various depositories.

In their policy of territorial expansion under the Hitler regime, the Germans systematically confiscated   reign documentation

---

*These depositories not subject to governmental security restrictions.

of possible value for German intelligence work and propagandistic purposes. Since many of the documents captured by the Germans before and during World War II were destroyed or have again become inaccessible to historical research, for the convenience of scholars a tentative listing of German publications based on German temporary possession of these documents has been appended to the bibliography. The listing of these documents in the bibliography does not, of course, imply any judgment by the War Documentation Project as to their authenticity.

The bibliography should be regarded as a preliminary survey of such information as could be gathered within a relatively short period of time as a by-product of the principal task of the War Documentation Project. Under the circumstances, the preparation of an evenly analytical, detailed survey was impossible. The nature of the sources of some of the information and the differences in the manner and state of organization of the materials in the various depositories have resulted in a compilation which, unfortunately, is very uneven in its treatment of different aspects of the same subject. Supplementary and more accurate information is being sought, and it may be possible to issue corrections and additions. Recommendations by users for improvement of the *Guide* will be welcomed. The War Documentation Project will greatly appreciate receiving comments and suggestions and, particularly, more detailed information derived from research on holdings of the depositories covered by the *Guide*. Communications may be sent c/o Bureau of Applied Social Research, Columbia University, 427 West 117th Street, New York 27, N. Y.

Conceived solely as an aid to research, no other consideration than possible research value has determined the selection of references to hitherto unpublished documents or to publications containing information about captured German documents. It is hoped that the *Guide* will prove helpful to those whose research interests require use of German documents, and will stimulate greater utilization of important documentary materials which have hitherto been neglected.

PART I

Books

Books

THE following is a list of books, organized alphabetically by author, which contain or refer to captured German documents. For those books which are available in the Library of Congress, the Library of Congress call number has been added in parentheses after the entry. In a few cases, books in Dutch have been included without any descriptive information. Copies of these have not been available in Washington; they are taken from a list of publications containing German documents furnished by The Netherlands State Institute for War-Documentation, Amsterdam.

Assmann, Kurt. *Deutsche Schicksalsjahre.* Wiesbaden: F. Brockhaus, 1950. The author had access to the captured records of the German Navy now in England.
(D 757.A8)

Belleman, Th. *Opdat wij niet vergeten.* Kampen: Kok, 1951. Numerous German documents on the relationship between the Dutch churches and the German occupation authorities, particularly on the intervention of the churches on behalf of Dutch Jews. (BX9474D4)

Bondy, L. W. *Racketeers of Hatred — Julius Streicher and the Jew Baiters International.* London, W. C. 2: Newman Wolsey Ltd., 1946. "Entirely new material included," according to the *Wiener Library Bulletin*, Vol. 1 (1946), 2.

Bouman, P. J. *De April-Meistakingen van 1943.* The Hague: Nijhoff, 1950. Numerous German documents on the general strike in the Netherlands in April—May 1943 in protest against return to German captivity of former members of Dutch armed forces. Of particular interest are the detailed reports of the Beauftragte des Reichskommissars for the various Dutch provinces (*Erfahrungsberichte ueber die Zeit des Ausnahmezustandes und des Polizeinotrechts*). (DJ287B6)

Cassou, Jacques. *Le Pillage par les Allemands des Oeuvres d'Art et des Bibliothèques.* Paris: Éditions du Centre, 1947. German documents on the looting of French works of art and libraries, particularly by the Einsatzstab Rosenberg. (N6841.C37)

Cohen, Adolf E. (ed.). *Vijf nota's van Mussert aan Hitler over de samenwerking van Duitschland en Nederland in een Bond van Germaansche Volkeren, 1940-1944.* The Hague: Nijhoff, 1947. Memoranda of Anton A. Mussert, leader of the Nationaal-Socialistische Beweging der Nederlanden (the Dutch Nazi party) to Hitler, August 27, 1940—November 17, 1944.
(DJ287.M88)

Cole, Hugh M. *The European Theater of Operations, The Lorraine Campaign.* (United States Army in World War II). United States, Department of the Army, Historical Division. Washington: Government Printing Office, 1950. Uses and cites Kriegstagebuecher of various German units and other captured German Army documents. (D769.A533, Vol. 3, P. 1)

Craven, Wesley Frank, and Cate, James Lea (eds.). *The Army Air Forces in World War II: Europe — Torch to Pointblank, August 1942 to December 1943.* United States, Office of Air Force History. Chicago: University of Chicago Press, 1949. Notes on pp. 759-836 contain references to captured German documents as well as to analyses and evaluations of captured German documents by the British, Canadian, and U.S. Air Forces. (D790.A47 Vol. II)

————. *The Army Air Forces in World War II: Europe — Argument to VE Day, January, 1944 to May, 1945.* Chicago: University of Chicago Press, 1951. The notes on pp. 811-909 contain references to various captured German documents, mainly of the German Air Force.

(D790.A47 Vol. III)

Deutsches Auslands-Institut, Stuttgart. "List of newspapers, principally representative of German groups outside of Germany." This is a photostat of a card catalog prepared in English in 1946. Newspapers of the DAI, organized alphabetically by country — city — name of paper.
(Z6956.G3D46, 1946a)

Feis, Herbert. *The Road to Pearl Harbor.* Princeton: Princeton University Press, 1950. Cites the individual exhibits introduced in the Tokyo War Crimes Trial, including the captured German documents cited there but not at Nuremberg.
(D757.F4)

Germany, Auswaertiges Amt. *Akten zur deutschen auswaertigen Politik, 1918-45,*

3

Serie D. Baden-Baden: Imprimerie Nationale, 1950-.
I. *Von Neurath zu Ribbentrop, Sept. 1937-Sept. 1938* (1950).
II. *Deutschland und die Tschechoslowakei, 1937-38* (1950). (JX691.A44)
English edition:
Documents on German Foreign Policy, 1918-1945. W a s h i n g t o n : Government Printing Office, 1949-.
I. *From Neurath to Ribbentrop, 1937-38* (1949).
II. *Germany and Czechoslovakia, 1937-38* (1949).
III. *Germany and the Spanish Civil War, 1936-39* (1950).
IV. *The Aftermath of Munich, 1938-39* (1951). (JX691.A45)
(NOTE: See Appendix 1 for special details.)

————. *Die Beziehungen zwischen Deutschland und der Sowjetunion, 1939-41.* Ed. Alfred Seidl. Tuebingen: H. Laupp, 1949. Captured documents from the German Foreign Office made available to Seidl as defense attorney at Nuremberg. A number of these have not been published in *Nazi-Soviet Relations, 1939-1941*; particularly documents dealing with the German attempt to improve Russo-Italian relations, the preparations for Molotov's visit to Berlin, and conversations between Ribbentrop and Skvartsev. (D754.R9G88,1941)

————. *Documents Secrets du Ministère des Affaires Étrangères d'Allemagne.* Trans. from the Russian by Madeleine and Michel Eristov. Paris: Éditions Paul Dupont, 1946.
I. *La Politique Allemande (1941-1943) Turquie.*
II. *La Politique Allemande (1937-1943) Hongrie.*
III. *La Politique Allemande (1936-1943) Espagne.*
These are documents captured and published by the Russians. (DD253.G386)
Vol. I has appeared in English under the title: *German Foreign Office Documents, German Policy in Turkey 1941-1943.* (DR479.G4A53)

————. *Dokumente und Materialien aus der Vorgeschichte des Zweiten Weltkrieges.* Moscow: Verlag fuer Fremdsprachige Literatur, 1948-49.
I. *Nov. 1937-38.*
II. *Das Archiv Dirksens, 1938-39.* (D785.G656)
German documents, also some Polish, Czech, and English documents. English

edition published under the title: *Documents and Materials Relating to the Eve of the Second World War.* (D785.G366)

————. *Nazi-Soviet Relations, 1939-1941.* Eds. R. J. Sontag and J. S. Beddie. Washington: Government Printing Office, 1948. Captured German documents in English, all but one from the German Foreign Office. (D754.R9G4, 1948)

The German edition was edited by E. M. Carroll and F. T. Epstein. It contains the German text of the documents with a full record of marginalia, accurate headings, index of names, some photographic reproductions, and more detailed notes. (D754.R9G4,1948b)

Supplementary note: for important documents on the Danube Conference of the winter of 1940 see Peter (pseud.?) "Die Sowjetunion und die Donaumuendung, Ende 1940. Dokumentarischer Bericht ueber die Bukarester Seedonaukonferenz," *Auswaertige Politik* XI (1944), 22-39. A copy is available in the New York Public Library.

————. "The record of collaboration of King Farouk of Egypt with the Nazis and their ally, the Mufti; the official Nazi records (of the Foreign Office) of the King's alliance and of the Mufti's plans for bombing Jerusalem and Tel Aviv." Memorandum submitted to the United Nations, June 1948. New York: Nation Associates, [1948]. Thirty-eight p., facsms. (DT82.5 G3)

In the Hoover Library; not in the Library of Congress.

Germany, Kriegsmarine, Oberkommando (OKM). *Fuehrer Conferences on Matters Dealing with the German Navy, 1939-1941.* United States, Department of the Navy, Washington: Department of the Navy, 1947. Seven vols. This is a translation of the Kriegstagebuch der Seekriegsleitung on the conferences of the Commander-in-Chief of the Navy with the Fuehrer. (D770.G42)

(English edition, *Fuehrer Conferences on Naval Affairs.* [London: Admiralty, 1947-48], has an eighth volume containing a name and subject index.)

Germany, Reichsministerium fuer Ruestung and Kriegsproduktion, Das Planungsamt. "Zahlenangaben ueber den Einsatz deutscher Frauen." (Microfilm print by the United States Strategic Bombing Survey.) A group of documents from the Planungsamt on various aspects of employment in German industry, May, 1944 — April,

1945. Includes a number of the Wochen-berichte of the Planungsamt.
(HD6148.A55)

——— "Soll-Ist-Vergleich." (Microfilm print by the United States Strategic Bombing Survey.) Tables and correspondence of the Planungsamt concerning production by German industry; totals for the years 1942 and 1943 and for each month of 1944.
(HD9506.G22A4)

Germany, Wehrmacht, Oberkommando (OKW). *Hitler Directs his War.* Ed. Felix Gilbert. New York: Oxford University Press, 1950. The secret records of Hitler's daily military conferences, selected and annotated from the manuscript in the library of the University of Pennsylvania. The book has detailed notes and a survey of the extant portions of the records of these conferences.   (D757.A5,1950)

Goebbels, Joseph. *The Goebbels Diaries,* 1942-1943. Ed. and trans. by Louis P. Lochner. Garden City: Doubleday and Co. Inc., 1948. Selections from the Goebbels diary at the Hoover Institute (*see* Part III).

Great Britain, Foreign Office. *Secret German documents seized during the raid on the Lofoten Islands, March 4, 1941, embodying instructions to the army on the control of the press and on collaboration with the Gestapo in dealing with Norwegian nationals.* London: H. M. Stationery Office, 1941. (Gt. Brit. Parliament. Cmd. 6270. Norway, 1941, No. 1.) Text in German and English. Four documents of Wehrmachtbefehlshaber Norwegen, 1940.
(D802.N7G7, 1941)

Harrison, Gordon A. *The European Theater of Operations, Cross-Channel Attack.* (United States Army in World War II.) United States, Department of the Army, Historical Division. Washington: Government Printing Office, 1951. Uses and cites in footnotes a large number of captured German military documents, particularly of German military commands in the West.
(D769.A533, Vol. 3, pt.2)

Hitler, Adolf, *Les lettres secrètes échangées par Hitler et Mussolini.* Paris: Editions du Pavois, 1946. Some of the letters exchanged by Hitler and Mussolini during the war years. Not a complete record of the correspondence.   (DD247.H5A37)

Holldack, Heinz. *Was wirklich geschah.* Munich: Nymphenburger Verlagshandlung, 1949. Gives full text of 65 of the Nuremberg documents in German. The cover-

ing note to document XXXXI (444-PS), p. 425, has not been published before and is very important.   (D751.H6)

Jannasch, W. *Deutsche Kirchendokumente.* Zuerich: Swiss Red Cross, 1946. See *Wiener Library Bulletin,* Vol. 2 (1948), 29.

Knout, David. *Le Résistance Juive en France 1940-1944.*
Paris: Editions du Centre, 1947. Centre du Documentation Juive Contemporaine; Série "Études et Monographies," No. 8. Contains reproductions, excerpts, and quotations from German documents apparently taken from police and military occupation files in France relating to resistance of the Jews to the Nazis.   (D810.J4K6)

Langer, William L., and Gleason, Everett S. *The Challenge to Isolation,* 1937-1940. New York: Harper and Brothers, Publishers, 1952. A few footnotes refer to unpublished documents from the German Foreign Office.

Lerner, Daniel. *Sykewar.* New York: George W. Stewart, Publisher, Inc., 1949. For information on the captured German documents of the Psychological Warfare Section of SHAEF see footnotes to the chapters and the description and lists on pp. 349-89.

Martienssen, Anthony K. *Hitler and his Admirals.* New York: E. P. Dutton, 1949. This book is based on and cites the various diaries of the German Navy (Kriegstagebuecher der Seekriegsleitung, Kriegstagebuch des Befehlshabers der Unterseeboote).   (D771.MC,1949)

Materialy do dziejów nowożytnych ziem zachodnich [Materials on the history of the western territories in modern times].
Vol. I. Stefan Golachowski, *Materialy do statystyki narodówosciowej Slaska Opolskiego z lat 1910-1939* [Materials concerning the statistics of nationalities of Upper Silesia, 1910-1939]. Vol. II. T. Bratus, St. Golachowski, W. Roszkowska, and B. Samitowska (eds.), *Polacy-Ewangelicy na Dolnym Slasku w XIX w. i ich postawa narodowo-spoleczna* [The Protestant Poles in Lower Silesia in the nineteenth century and their national-social behavior]. Posen-Breslau: Instytut Zachodni [Western Institute], 1950. Documents from the Prussian State Archives at Breslau and other depositories in Silesia, published in German with Polish notes, with statistics and other information concerning the nationality problems of Silesia. Volume II contains documents from the

twentieth as well as the nineteenth century.

Mehnert, Klaus, and Schulte, Heinrich (eds.). *Deutschland-Jahrbuch* 1949. Essen: West-Verlag, 1949. Chapter 45: A survey of the fate of German libraries, pp. 380-88.

Poliakow, L. *La condition des Juifs en France sous l'occupation italienne.* Paris: Éditions du Centre, 1946.   (D810.J4P615)

————. *L'Étoile Jaune.* Paris: Éditions du Centre, 1949. Centre de Documentation Juive Contemporaine, No. 2. Quotations, excerpts, and reproductions of SS documents concerning the Jews, mainly from files in France.   (D810.J4,P617)

Pousset, David. *Le Pitrène rit pas.* Paris: Éditions du Pavois, 1948. Includes a number of Nazi documents now in Allied possession, including one from the French General Commissariat for Jewish Questions, according to *Wiener Library Bulletin,* Vol. 8 (1949), 14.

Rossi, Angelo. *Deux ans d'alliance Germano-Soviétique.* Paris: A. Fayard, 1949. Quotes, cites, and reproduces photographically a number of captured documents from the German Foreign Office not published elsewhere.   (D754.R9R68)

Semmler, Rudolf. *Goebbels —The Man next to Hitler.* London: Westhouse, 1947. Diary of Semmler of the Propaganda Ministry about Goebbels' activities in the ministry. December 31, 1940 — April 17, 1945. The diary was given by Semmler's wife to Helge Knudsen and was brought to England.   (DD247.G6S4)

Sijes, B. A. *De Razzia van Rotterdam,* 10-11 *November* 1944. The Hague: Nijhoff, 1951. A study of the great German slave-labor hunting operation in Rotterdam in November, 1944. Contains order of the Office of the Field Security Police (Feldkommandantur) Nr. 724 of November 9, 1944. See List of Annexes, p. 278.

Sijes, B. A., and de Jong, L. *De Februaristaking* 1941. This book is to be published by Nijhoff (The Hague) and will include German documents on the revolt in Amsterdam in February, 1941, against German anti-Semitic outrages.

Steward, John S. *Sieg des Glaubens.* Zuerich: Thomas-Verlag, 1946. The Allies captured the files of the Gauleitung Baden (Gauleiter Robert Wagner) in Strasbourg. The documents are largely Gestapo reports on the sentiments of the people.

Lage- und Stimmungsberichte der Kreisleiter an die Gauleitung and of the Kreisschulleiter an die Gauschulleitung; Anweisungen und Berichte des Reichssicherheitshauptamtes (and its local offices.) Berichte an den Beauftragten des Fuehrers fuer die Ueberwachung der gesamten geistigen und weltanschaulichen Erziehung der NSDAP. SD Berichte. The captured documents date mainly to 1942-45; some go back to 1939. The book gives the text and excerpts of documents dealing with opposition to the regime by the religious element, particularly the Catholics. Also samples of other important categories of documents as listed above.
   (BX1536.S75)

Tauw, H. C. *Het verzet der Hervormde Kerk.* The Hague: Boekencentrum, 1946.

Trevor-Roper, Hugh R. *The Last Days of Hitler.* 2nd. revised ed. New York: The Macmillan Company, 1949. Used captured German documents; gives no list of them but explains his investigative technique.
   (DD247.H6T7,1949)

Vries, Ph. de. *Geschiedenis van het verzet der artsen in Nederland.* Haarlem: Tjeenk Willink, 1949.

Watson, Mark Skinner. *The War Department, Chief of Staff: Pre-war Plans and Preparations.* (United States Army in World War II.) United States, Department of the Army, Historical Division. Washington: Government Printing Office, 1950. See note 79, pp. 359-60, for citation of "Notes for a Report" of the Oberkommando der Wehrmacht, Wehrmachtfuehrungsstab, L (IK-OP) of 14 December 1941 concerning the publication of secret American military plans in the *Chicago Tribune.*   (D769.A533, Vol. 4 P. 1)

Weil, Dr. Joseph. *Contribution à l'histoire des Camps d'Internement.* Paris: Éditions du Centre, 1946. Contains some German documents and French documents on the internment and deportations of French Jews.   (D805F8W4)

Wielek, H. *De Oorlog die Hitler won.* Amsterdam: Amsterdamse Boek-en Courantenmij, 1947.   (D802N4N48)

Zielinski, Henryk. *Polacy i Polskość ziemi Zlotowskiej w latach* 1918-1939 [Poles and Polishdom in the county of Flatow in the years of 1918-1939]. Posen: Instytut Zachodni [Western Institute], 1949. This study is based largely on local German archives of the Flatow area. A considerable number of documents is cited in footnotes and three are reprinted in German in full. (DD491.069Z5)

Appendix 1—Files of the Auswaertige Amt

A listing of German Foreign Office documents now in the custody of the United States, Great Britain, and France will be found in *Documents on German Foreign Policy*, 1918-1945, Volume II, pp. 1024-29. Aside from those documents, properly a part of the Foreign Office files, the following items should be noted.

No.	Description	Period	Bundles
49	Reichstag Untersuchungsausschuss ueber die Weltkriegsverantwortung	1914-1926	20
53	Head of the Auslandsorganisation in the Foreign Ministry, (This was actually a Nazi Party office, its head was a Gauleiter)	1937-1943	40
162	Handakten Epp (Reichsstatthalter of Bavaria, Head of the NSDAP Kolonialpolitisches Amt)	1918-1945	36
163	Handakten Frank (Generalgouverneur des Generalgouvernement)	1918-1945	86
164	Handakten Speer (Reichsminister fuer Ruestung und Kriegsproduktion)	1936-1945	18
165	Ibero-Amerikanisches Institut	1933-1945	69
166	Alte Reichskanzlei	1920-1933	5565 files
167	Neue Reichskanzlei	1933-1945	1630 files
168	Praesidialkanzlei	1919-1940	125
169	Kanzlei des Stellvertreters des Fuehrers	1933-1942	166 files
170	Adjutantur des Fuehrers	1935-1940	828 files
171	Party offices	1930	15
172	Various documents of foreign origin	1912-1945	95

Appendix 2—Scandinavian document publications relating to the German occupation of Denmark and Norway, 1940-1945

1. DENMARK

Denmark, Rigsdagen, Folketinget. Vol. I. *Betaenkning til Folketinget.* Vols II and IV. *Beretning til Folketinget.* Kobenhavn: J. H. Schultz, 1945-. Report of the Danish Parliamentary Investigating Commission on the German occupation of Denmark, 1940-1945. Altogether nine vols. planned. Contains numerous German documents in both the original and Danish translations, some facsimiles. Almost all of these documents are communications between the Danish Government and German occupation authorities or the German Foreign Office. (D763.D4A45)

2. NORWAY

Norway, Utenriksdepartement. *Norges forhold til Sverige under krigen* 1940-45. Vol. I (to June 1940), Oslo, 1947. Vol. II (to October 1941), Oslo, 1948. Vol III (1941-45), Oslo, 1950. Volume I contains 69 documents from German Foreign Office files on German-Swedish relations, April—June 1940; problems in German-Swedish relations arising out of the German occupation of Norway, particularly the question of transit of goods and men from Germany across Sweden to Norway, and the proposed neutralization of Narvik. (D754.N6A52)
Innstilling fra Undersokelseskommisjonen av 1945. Utg. av Stortinget, Del. I, II & Bil. 1, 2, 3. Oslo, 1946-47. Report of the Norwegian Parliamentary Investigating Commission on the German occupation of Norway, 1940-1945. (Not in the Library of Congress.) According to a note by W. Hubatsch in *Historische Zeitschrift*, Vol. 171 (1951), 217-218, this publication contains a number of captured German documents relating to the German occupation of Norway.

3. SWEDEN

The above-mentioned bibliographical note in the *Historische Zeitschrift* mentions that in the series, *Handlinger roerande Sveriges politik under andra vaerldskriget* (Stockholm, 1947-), published by the Swedish Foreign Office, a number of German documents are cited or reproduced. The following titles have appeared:
1. *Transiteringsfrdgan Juni-December* 1940 (1947). (D754.S8A5,1940a)
2. *Transiteringsfrdgor och daermed sammanhaenyande spoersmdl April-Juni* 1940 (1947). (D754.S8A5,1940)
3. *Foerspelet till det tyska angreppet pd Danmark och Norge den 9 April 1940* (1947). (Not in the Library of Congress.)
4. *Frdgor i samband med norska regeringens vistelse utanfoer Norge 1940-1943* (1948). (D754.S8A55)

NOTE: W. Hubatsch is quite critical of the presentation and selection of captured German documents in all of these Scandinavian document publications, particularly in regard to identification and editing. See also Hubatsch's article, "Die Skandinawischen Weissbuecher," in *Aussenpolitik*, Vol. 1, No. 2 (1951), 117-25.

PART II

Periodicals

9

Periodicals

THIS is a compilation of information on captured German documents found in various periodicals. The War Documentation Project does not vouch for the accuracy of statements in these periodicals. Information on related groups of documents scattered among the various periodicals, can be pulled together through the use of the index.

Aktion (Frankfurt a.M., Margarete Buber-Neumann, publ.)

No. 9 (1951), pp. 38-42.

Egon Merker, "Ehemalige deutsche Reichs-archive."

Brief listing of the fate of various large German archives.

The remainder of the archives of the Geheime Staatsarchiv, Berlin-Dahlem, is now in the Berliner Hauptarchiv, in Western Berlin. It includes:

Reichsfinanzministerium, almost complete;

Reichswirtschaftsministerium, some;

Reichsministerium fuer Wissenschaft, Erziehung, und Volksbildung, some;

Reichsministerium fuer Kirchliche Angelegenheiten, some;

Volksgerichtshof, some;

Reichskulturkammer, some.

The author states that there is almost no information on the fate of the former Heeresarchiv Wien. Some of the collection is believed to be in Russian hands; much was lost in the war.

The Russians obtained large parts of the files of the Reichspropagandaministerium, including the "Schnelldienst" which contained many of the most important files. The Russians are also supposed to have the files of the Reichspressekammer.

The Zentralarchiv of the Deutsche Demokratische Republik (Soviet Zone) in Potsdam has the files of the Deutsche Volkspartei, Deutschnationale Volkspartei, and the Stahlhelm.

The archives of the Sozialdemokratische Partei Deutschlands (SPD) and of the Marx-Engels-Archiv are in the International Institute for Social History, Amsterdam.

The American Archivist

Published by the National Archives of the United States   (CD3020.A 45)

Vol. 9 (1946), 89-91.

News Note: The following note under the title, "The Germans and their archives" was submitted to the editors by Capt. Marvin C. Ross, USMCR, formerly deputy advisor to the Monuments, Fine Arts, and Archives Sub-commission at SHAEF . . . now returned to the staff of Walters Art Gallery in Baltimore, quoting from a German pamphlet, ca. 1942, prepared by a committee appointed by the Minister of Education of Baden for the preservation of German War Documents. According to Capt. Ross, these instructions as regards the Archives of Baden and Alsace were carried out pretty thoroughly . . .

Vol. 9 (1946), 110-127.

Oliver W. Holmes. "The National Archives and the Protection of Records in War Areas." Gives the background of American and Allied activity in German archives. P. 123: German Ministerial Records concentrated at the Kassel Collecting Point.

Vol. 9 (1946), 261.

National Archives gets from the White House Hitler's marriage certificate, private will, and last political testament.

Vol. 9 (1946), 391-93.

Notes: "Description of the Prussian Privy State Archives (Preussisches Geheimes Staatsarchiv) in Berlin-Dahlem, as of Aug. 1945." Fate of the records:

Lost in the war were the general map collection, the collection of seals, the land record of Mark Brandenburg, and other older materials.

Captured by the Poles and apparently taken away were the holdings of the library.

The bulk of the records (three-fifths of the State Archives — 180,000 bundles) was stored in two salt mines in Stassfurt and Schoenebeck near Magdeburg in the Russian Zone.

Ten thousand packages were stored in an anti-aircraft tower in the Soviet sector of Berlin.

Stored in the mines also were the collections of material, working papers, and other manuscripts of the:

1. Institut fuer Archivalische Wissenschaft,

2. Kaiser Wilhelm-Institut fuer Deutsche Geschichte,

3. Hansischer Geschichtsverein,

4. Zentralstelle fuer Nachkriegsgeschichte,

5. Institut fuer Heimatforschung der Universitaet Berlin (Schneidemuehl), and apparently some others.

Vol. 10 (1947), 104.

U. S. military authorities have the membership records of the NSDAP transferred to Berlin Document Center.

Vol. 11 (1948), 82.

National Archives received:

1) Records of the German-American Bund and of the law firm of Hutz and Joslin (attorneys for IG Farben).

2) Recordings of speeches of Axis leaders and other propaganda material, 1939-1945, seized by American forces (from the War Dept.).

Vol. 14 (Feb. 1951).

Lester Born: "The Ministerial Collecting Center, near Kassel, Germany."

American Historical Review   (E717.A57)

Vol. 54 (1949), 973.

"Records of the Monuments, Fine Arts, and Archives Section of the U. S. Office of Military Government for Germany (OMGUS), 1946-47, consisting of questionnaires, reports, and about 1,800 photographs of war-damaged cultural institutions and monuments in the U. S. Zone of Germany" are kept at the United States National Archives. (This is a file organized alphabetically by city.)

Vol. 55 (1949), 262.

Negative micro-copies, positive prints of which may be purchased, have been made by the National Archives of the papers of Generals Hans von Seeckt and Wilhelm Groener.

For listings of the contents of these films, see The National Archives, *List of File Micro-copies of the National Archives* (Washington, 1950), pp. 57-60.

Vol. 56 (1950) 34-57.

Lester Born, "Archives and Libraries of Post-War Germany."

A survey of the archive and library situation in Germany since the end of the war. Contains valuable references to other articles on the subject. See entries particularly under *Der Archivar.*

Vol. 57 (1951), 77-90.

Henry Cord Meyer, "German Economic Relations with Southeastern Europe, 1870-1914." Some of the footnotes cite the Groener draft autobiography in the Groener papers in the National Archives (from the Heeresarchiv).

Der Archivar (Published by the Staatsarchiv Duesseldorf for the Verein Deutscher Archivare)

Available in the Periodicals Room of the Library of Congress, no catalog number. Unbound.

Vol. 1 (1948) cc. 51-68.

Situation reports on Staats-, Stadt-, und Kirchenarchive in the United States Zone of Germany.

Vol. 1 (1948) cc. 67-71.

The Archives in Southwest Germany after World War II.

Vol. 1 (1948) c. 73.

List of Archives and parts of Archives now located in Zonenarchiv at Goslar. Among them are parts of:

Staatsarchiv Koenigsberg
Ritterschaftsarchive Kurland und Livland
Staatsarchiv Anhalt
Landesarchiv Luebben
Stadt-und Kirchenarchiv Prenzlau
Stadtarchiv Reval
Gauarchiv Koenigsberg
Staatsarchiv Schwerin.

Vol. 1 (1948) c. 74.

C. A. F. Meekings, "Rueckgabe von Archiven an Polen." Describes the controversial matter of the transfer or return to the custody of the Polish Government of certain archives of Danzig, Stettin, etc., from the British Zone.

Vol. 1 (1948) c. 97.

Gerichtsaktenarchiv der deutschen Kriegsmarine is now under the administrative control of the Oberstaatsanwalt, Flensburg.

Vol. 1 (1948) cc. 97-134 and 169-178.

"Kriegsschutz- und Rueckfuehrungsmassnahmen und deren Erfahrungen sowie Verluste der Archive in der britischen Zone." Parts I and II.

Vol. 1 (1948) cc. 138-140.

A. von Brandt, "Schicksalsfragen deutscher Archive." Presents the German argument against the transfer from the British Zone to the Polish Government of certain archives belonging to Danzig, Stettin, etc., as reported in the brief item by C. A. F. Meekings entered above.

Vol. 1 (1948) cc. 139-143.

Sources for the history of the "Ostvertriebenen." Contains references to many important records pertaining to the Banat which are now collected in the Vienna Haus-, Hof-

und Staatsarchiv. Several studies are under way on the history of the Volksdeutsche in Bessarabia, Bulgaria, Yugoslavia, and Transylvania.

Vol. 3 (1950), cc. 27-34.

H. M. Maschke, "Die Deutschen Akten und das Kriegsrecht." A discussion of the legal status of the "captured" German records of World War II.

Vol. 3 (1950), cc. 38-38 and Vol. 4 (1951), cc. 1-14.

Wolfgang Mommsen, "Deutsche Archivalien im Ausland." Part I is a detailed discussion of the disposition and location of captured German archives in Allied hands. Part II deals with the files of the Auswaertige Amt.

Vol. 3 (1950), cc. 78-94.

"Die Lage der deutschen Ostarchive." Additional information about preservation and location of archives now located in the Polish-occupied German territories east of the Oder-Neisse, the Soviet Zone of Germany, and Berlin.

Vol. 3 (1950), cc. 104-122.

Wilhelm Rohr, "Die zentrale Lenkung deutscher Archivschutzmassnahmen im Zweiten Weltkrieg." An associate of the Generaldirektor of the Preussische Staatsarchive and the Reichsarchiv, Dr. Ernst Zipfel, describes the various measures attempted during the war to establish and to carry out a uniform policy for the protection of German archives against air attacks and capture by enemy troops.

Vol. 3 (1950), cc. 153-177.

"Aktenhaltung und Archivgutpflege im Reichsarbeitsdienst." Detailed description of the identifying symbols and the filing system of the German Labor Service. Also contains information on the location and the disposition of the Arbeitsdienst files in April and May of 1945.

Vol. 3. (1950), cc. 177-179.

"Heeresarchiv Potsdam." Contains the following information on the fate of the Heeresarchiv holdings:

1. All records of the old Brandenburg-Prussian Army and of the Reichswehr are destroyed. A few "Nachlaesse" and war diaries of World War II are now in Allied hands.
   (See U. S. National Archives.)
2. The fate of the Heeresarchiv Vienna is unknown.
3. The archives of the former Saxonian Army (1860-1920) are now in Soviet hands.
4. The Stuttgart and Munich Army Ar-

chives have been salvaged and are now in Hauptarchiv Munich.

Vol. 3 (1950), cc. 191-196.

"Nachrichten ueber Archivalien in der Tschechoslowakei." Contains the following information:

1. Files of the Reichsarchiv in Berlin-Dahlem were located in Friedland, CSR.
2. The card files and records of the former Deputy Protector of Bohemia and Moravia, Karl H. Frank, and of the Sudetendeutsche Partei were taken to Prague and are now kept in the Czechoslovak Ministry of the Interior.
3. Also seized by the Czechoslovakian Government were German plans for the "Aussiedlung" of the Czech population to Russia.
4. A special search team of the Prague National Library seized large holdings of books confiscated by the SS from Jewish communities, etc.
5. In Kuttenberg, CSR, a "Historisch-geographisches Institut" of the SS was located whose files were apparently evacuated to Germany shortly before the end of the war and thus far have not been found.
6. Most of the archives seized by the Germans in the Ukraine, White Russia, and the Baltic States were taken to Troppau, CSR. There they were partly lost while other parts were recovered by the Czech Government and presumably returned to their places of origin.

Cahiers d'Histoire de la Guerre

Publication du Comité d'Histoire de la Guerre, Paris

No. 1 (1949), pp. 44-46.

J. Mady, "Fonds d'Archives concernant la Deuxième Guerre Mondiale Conservés aux Archives Nationales."

The following files have been deposited in the French National Archives. They are closed to the public for 50 years:

Militärbefehlshaber in Frankreich (found in the Hotel Majestic)
Militärbefehlshaber in Belgien und Nordfrankreich
Archives of the Propaganda-Staffel Paris (found in the Hotel Majestic)
Files of the Gruppe Kultur und Schulen (found in the Hotel Majestic)
Archives of the Devisenschutzkommando
Archives of the NSDAP, Gau Baden. also for Alsace during the occupation (1937-1944).

No. 4 (1950), pp. 72-77.

"Les intentions allemandes se précisent (Juillet, 1940).

Translation into French of two German documents: [Hemmen] to Wiehl, 18 July 1940 (No. 26).

Wiehl to Hemmen, 20 July 1940.

Documents located at the Centre de Documentation Juive Contemporaine.

No. 4 (1950), pp. 107-110.

Nicole R. Michel - Dansai, "Les Archives de la Haute Cour de Justice; II. Archives d'Origine Allemande."

Three groups of German documents at the Haute Cour de Justice.

1. Some documents of Abetz used in the Abetz Trial.
2. Documents of the Militaerbefehlshaber Frankreich.
3. Copies of documents from the German Foreign Office concerning relations between Germany and Vichy.

Department of State Bulletin. (JK 232 A33)

Vol. 12 (1945), 537-538.

Press release of 30 March 1945:

The Department of State announced that according to reliable information gathered by the Allied Governments, the Nazi Government has well-developed, well-arranged postwar plans for the perpetuation of Nazi doctrines and domination.

"This Government is now in possession of several volumes of German plans on infiltration via schools to foreign countries . . ."

Vol. 14 (1946), 285-89.

Consultation among the American Republics with Respect to the Argentine Situation (Washington, 1946). (Contains excerpts and summaries but no full document texts.)

"An enormous volume of documents of the defeated enemy" producing evidence of Argentine complicity with the Nazis. Documentary evidence on Argentine-Nazi complicity; Hellmuth Mission. (State Dept. Publication 2473.)

Vol. 14 (1946), 278-281.

Sexton Bradford, "Deutsche Auslandspropaganda." Note with the article states: "With this article the Department of State is initiating publication of documentation secured from official German Government files as a result of the surrender of Germany . . . Publication of other materials will follow." Based on captured German documents, but does not cite directly.

Vol. 14 (1946), 311-313.

Sections of Standardthesen und Richtlinien fuer die deutsche Auslandspropaganda which were issued by the Chief of Propaganda in the German Foreign Ministry, Dr. Megerle, dated 8 Feb. 1943, 29 Dec. 1941, 4 Jan. 1942, and 19 Mar. 1942.

[A compilation of all these and others was published by the German Foreign Ministry on 12 May 1943, under the title of *Zusammenstellung der Standardthesen und Richtlinien fuer die Deutsche Auslandspropaganda.* The book was marked "Nur fuer den Dienstgebrauch"; a captured copy is now in the Library of Congress. (DD254.AS, 1943)].

Vol. 14 (1946), 365-369.

Excerpts from "Basic Postulates and General Themes for German Propaganda abroad", No. 20: Instructions for propaganda to England, dated 11 Feb. 1942 and 10 Mar. 1942.

Vol. 14 (1946) 413-427.

Publication of excerpts of 15 documents concerning the relations of the Spanish Government to the European Axis.

Full text of the documents published as No. 2483, European Series 8, Division of Research and Publication, U. S. Department of State: *The Spanish Government and the Axis.*   (0754.S7U5,1946)

Vol. 14 (1946), 459-466.

Documents on the Mission of Sumner Welles in 1940:

(a) General directions by Hitler for the conduct of conversations with Sumner Welles, 29 Feb. 1940, pp. 259-260.
(b) Memorandum by Schmidt (interpreter), 4 March 1940, on Goering-Welles conversation in Karinhall on 3 March 1940, pp. 460-466.

Vol. 14 (1946), 699-703, 721.

German documents on the invasion of Norway, 1940, secured from German Government files.

Memorandum by Hewel, 13 April 1940, on conversation between Hitler and Scheel (Norwegian minister) in presence of Ribbentrop and Habicht, 13 April 1940.

Vol. 14 (1946), 936-940.

German documents on Hitler's plans for the future of Norway and Denmark, 1942.

Memorandum of Woermann, 17 Feb. 1942.
Memorandum of Quisling, 10 Feb. 1942.
Lammers to Quisling, 17 Sept. 1942.
Memorandum of von Grundherr, 8 Oct. 1942.

Vol. 14 (1946), 948-986, 989.

German documents on Hungary, secured from German Government files.

Memorandum of Woermann, 16 Sept. 1936.
Memorandum of Erich Kordt, 21 Sept. 1938.

Ribbentrop to Erdmannsdorff (No. 552), 15 June 1941.

Weber (Ministerbuero) to Foreign Office (No. 75), 17 Jan. 1942, on conversation of Ribbentrop with Horthy in presence of Bardossy on Jan. 6-9, 1942.

Ribbentrop to Veesenmayer (No. 93), 19 Jan. 1942.

Vol. 14 (1946), 1038-1041, 1050.

German documents on relations with Japan.

Memorandum of Weizsaecker (St. S. No. 648), 26 Aug. 1939.

Memorandum of Weizsaecker (St. S. No. 734), 18 Sept. 1939; enclosure: Oshima to Ribbentrop, 26 Aug. 1939.

Ott to Ribbentrop (No. 594), 19 June 1940; memorandum on this by Wiehl, 20 June 1940.

Braeuer to Ribbentrop, 10:00 P.M., 10 April, 1940 (telephone).

Memorandum of Hewel, 13 April 1940, on conversation between Hitler and Hagelin (of the Quisling Govt.) in presence of Ribbentrop and Habicht, 13 April 1940.

Ribbentrop to Ott (No. 942), July 1, 1941 (Secret).

"Conferences with Axis Leaders:"

I. Vol. 14 (1946), 1103-1107, 1124.

Memorandum of Schmidt, 14 May 1941, on conversation of Mussolini with Ribbentrop in the presence of Ciano at the Palazzo Venezia on May 13, 1940; Foreign Minister's Memorandum 31/41.

II. Vol. 15 (1946), 57-63.

Memorandum of Schmidt, 2 May 1942, on conversation of Hitler with Mussolini in the presence of Ribbentrop and Ciano at Salzburg on 29 Apr. 1942, Fuehrer's Memorandum 15/42.

III. Vol. 15 (1946), 197-201, 236.

Memorandum of Schmidt, 8 May 1943, on conversation of Hitler with Laval in the presence of Ribbentrop and Bastianini on 29 Apr. 1943, Fuehrer's Memorandum 31/43.

IV. Vol. 15 (1946), pp. 607-614, 639.

Memorandum of Schmidt, 20 July 1943, on conversation of Hitler with Mussolini in the presence of Bastianini, Mackensen, Hewel, Alfieri, Keitel, Ambrosio, Rintelen, and Warlimont in northern Italy on 19 July 1943.

V. Vol. 15 (1946), 695-699.

Memorandum of Sonnleithner, 23 Apr. 1944, on conversation of Hitler with Mussolini in the presence of Ribbentrop, Keitel, Rahn, Wolff, Toussaint, Jandl, Dollmann, Graziani, Mazzolini, Anfuso, and Morera at Salzburg on 22 April 1944, from 11 A.M. to 1

P.M. Fuehrer's Memorandum 18/44.

VI. Vol. 15 (1946), 1040-1047, 1061.

Memorandum of Sonnleithner on conversation of Hitler with Mussolini in the presence of Ribbentrop, Keitel, Rahn, Graziani, Anfuso, and Mazzolini at Salzburg on 23 Apr. 1944 from 12-2 P.M., Fuehrer's Memorandum 20/44.

"Conferences with Japanese Representatives:"

I. Vol. 15 (1946), 399-403, 427.

Memorandum of Gottfriedsen, 19 Apr. 1943, on conversation of Ribbentrop with Oshima and Nomura at Fuschl on 18 Apr. 1943.

II. Vol. 15 (1946), 480-486.

Memorandum of Gottfriedsen on conversation of Ribbentrop with Oshima in the presence of Maj. Gen. Okamoto at Fuschl on 19 May 1943, Foreign Minister's Memorandum 32/43.

III. Vol. 15 (1946), 564-569.

Memorandum of Gottfriedsen, 28 Nov. 1943, on Ribbentrop's conversation with Oshima in Berlin on 28 Nov. 1943.

Memorandum, 11 Dec. 1943, on Ribbentrop-Oshima conversation in Berlin on 11 Dec. 1943.

Memorandum of Hewel on conversation of Hitler with Oshima in the presence of Ribbentrop on 22 Jan. 1944, Fuehrer's Memorandum 2/44.

Vol. 15 (1946), p. 691.

Announcement of the intention of the U. S. Department of State to publish an authoritative collection of German Foreign Ministry and other official documents. Dr. Raymond J. Sontag, Univ. of California, to be the Director of the German War Documents Project.

Vol. 16 (1947), 211.

State Department announcement of the control of documents removed from German diplomatic establishment in the U. S.; further information on the German War Documents Project. These "records are now in joint Anglo-American custody in Berlin, where for over a year a team of specialists has been microfilming the more important documents. . . ." and announcement of the British co-editor: Mr. John W. Wheeler-Bennett (Oxford).

Vol. 16 (1947), 1136.

Announcement of May 19, 1947, re: cooperation of French scholars on the German War Documents Project.

Vol. 17 (1947), 944.

"Publication plans for Captured German

Documents" (Statement by the Secretary of State).

Deutsche Rundschau (Essen)

Vol. 76 (1950).

Reginald H. Phelps, "Aus den Groener-Dokumenten." A series of articles with the following subtitles:
- pp. 530-41. "Groener, Ebert und Hindenburg."
- pp. 616-25. "Die Aussenpolitik der O.H.L. bis zum Friedensvertrag."
- pp. 735-49. "Bayern und Reich."
- pp. 830-40. "Das Baltikum 1919."
- pp. 915-22. "Der Fall Scheringer-Ludin-Wendt."
- pp. 1013-1022. "Die Briefe an Alarich von Gleich."

Vol. 77 (1951), 19-31.

"Das S.A.-Verbot und der Sturz des Kabinetts Bruening."

A very careful, detailed review of Groener papers deposited with the Heeresarchiv Potsdam and now at the National Archives, Washington, D. C., mentions that of the 290 items originally deposited at the Heeresarchiv only 254 were taken to the United States.

Europa-Archiv   (D839.E86)

(Frankfurt a. M.)

Vol. 4 (1949), 2585-90.

Rudolf Holzhausen, "Die Quellen zur Erforschung der Geschichte des 'Dritten Reiches' von 1938 bis 1945." An article on the fate of the German archives.

Jewish Social Studies.

Conference on Jewish Relations, New York

Vol. 13 (1951), pp. 235-50.

Philip Friedman, "American Jewish Research and Literature on the Jewish Catastrophe of 1939-1945." This article contains a detailed survey of the holdings of the following institutions:
- Institute of Jewish Affairs.
- Yiddish Scientific Institute (YIVO), formerly of Vilna, now in New York.

There is also much information on research and libraries in this field.

Journal of Central European Affairs   (D1 J57)

Vol. 7 (1948), 394-405.

Alma Luckau, "Kapp Putsch—Success or Failure." Article based on the Seeckt papers in the National Archives; contains translations of two of the Seeckt documents relating to the Kapp Putsch.

Journal of Documentation
Association of Special Libraries and Information Bureaus, London.

Vol. 8 (1947), 99-106.

Kenneth S. Garside. "An Intelligence Library in Germany."

An account of the establishment of a library of German documents, books and periodicals for the use of the Intelligence Section, British Army of the Rhine, at Herford, Germany. Library consists mainly of sources on German armed forces and NSDAP.

Of interest is the manner in which the Library of Congress system was somewhat expanded and adapted to the need of providing a sufficiently large number of symbols for the various organizations of the Wehrmacht and the NSDAP.

Journal of Modern History   (D1 J6)

Vol. 20 (1948), 183-186.

Richard A. Humphrey, "War-born Microfilm Holdings of the Department of State." A general account of the source, nature, and disposition of captured German Foreign Ministry documents.

Vol. 21 (1949), 28-34.

George W. F. Hallgarten, "General Hans von Seeckt and Russia, 1920-1922." This article is based on and cites the Seeckt papers now in the U. S. National Archives and thus gives some clues as to their contents.

Vol. 23 (1951), 58-71.

George Fischer, "Vlassov and Hitler." Contains the German text of a conference of Hitler with the German military leaders on June 8, 1943.

Der Monat

(Berlin-Dahlem)

1948, No. 1, 43-50.

Julius Epstein, "Der Seeckt-Plan: Aus unveroeffentlichten Dokumenten." Contains full text of the following documents from the Seeckt papers in the U. S. National Archives:
- Graf Brockdorff-Rantzau's Promemoria-Ostpolitik, July 1922, and Seeckt's comment on it, dated Sept. 1922.
- Letter of Hauptmann Tschunke to Rabenau, dated February 1939.

1949, No. 1, 26-38.

Robert W. Kempner, "Kampf gegen die Kirche."

Excerpts from the unpublished diary of Alfred Rosenberg. Entries made between 1936 and 1943 reveal Rosenberg's uncompromising attitude toward the churches and his proposals to deal with them as harshly as possible. These diary excerpts were not available to Lang and Schenck for their book: *Portrait eines Menschheitsverbrechers* (St. Gallen, 1947).

Le Monde Juif

Revue du Centre de Documentation Juive Contemporaine

The French periodical, *Le Monde Juif*, contains numerous publications of German documents, mostly on the treatment of Jews in France and the other Nazi-occupied countries. Documents of this kind may be found in virtually every issue of this periodical of which the Library of Congress has a complete set.   (DS 101. M 68)

The following are examples of significant document publications:

Vol. 1 (1947), no. 5, pp. 2-3.
"Le pillage de la France révélé par des documents allemands."

Vol. 1 (1947), No. 9 - 10, pp. 2-4.
"Un congrès qui n'a pas eu lieu," (Documents on the planned international anti-Jewish congress at Cracow, July 1944).

Vol. 3 (1948), No. 14, pp. 7-12; No. 15, pp. 13-18.
George Wellers, "Prélude aux déportations des Juifs de France."

Vol. 4 (1949), No. 21, pp. 11-16; No. 22-23, pp. 6-10.
George Wellers, "Les rafles du 16 et 17 Juillet 1942 dans la région parisienne."

Vol. 4 (1949), No. 24, pp. 7-11; No. 25, pp. 5-7; No. 26, pp. 5-9.
Jacques Sabille, "Comment furent sauvés les Juifs du Danmark."

Vol. 5 (1950), No. 27, pp. 4-7; No. 28, pp. 8-11.
Jacques Sabille, "Documents sur l'action suédoise en faveur des Juifs de Hollande, de Norvège et de Hongrie."

Vol. 5 (1950), No. 30, pp. 4-7, No. 31, pp. 6-8.
Jacques Sabille, "Le sauvetage des Juifs bulgares pendant la deuxième Guerre Mondiale."

Vol. 5 (1950), No. 38, pp. 7-9.
Jacques Sabille, "Académie des Huns." (La Hohe Schule de Hitler et de Rosenberg.) Deals with the Institut zur Erforschung der Judenfrage, Frankfurt a. M.

Vol. 5 (1950), No. 32, pp. 5-9; No. 34-35, pp. 7-10; No. 36, pp. 4-7; No. 37, pp. 5-8.
Michael Mazor, "Les archives de Rosenberg"

I.   Le totalitarianisme hitlérien
II.   Antijudéisme - arme secrète nazie

III. Antijudéisme - gage de la résurrection de nazisme
IV.   Bagatelles pour un massacre
V.   Rosenberg, grand chef du pillage.

Vol. 5 (1951), No. 39, pp. 5-9.
Jacques Sabille, "Le sauvetage des Juifs finlandais."

Vol. 5 (1951), No. 40, pp. 6-8.
Jacques Sabille, "Le sauvetage des Juifs détenus dans les camps nazis."

Vol. 5 (1951), No. 43, pp. 3-7; No. 44, pp. 3-6; No. 45, pp. 3-8.
Michael Mazor, "La justice Hitlérienne"
I.   (Missing)
II.   L'arbitraire, base du système judiciaire nazi
III. Tribunaux nazis, instruments de meurtres judiciaires
IV.   Les Magistrats-bourreaux et leurs victimes.

Vol. 5 (1951), No. 46-47, pp. 5-8; No. 48, pp. 6-10.
Jacques Sabille, "L'attitude des Italiens envers les Juifs persécutés en Croatie."

Nederland in Oorlogstijd

(Published in Amsterdam by the Netherlands State Institute for War-Documentation)

The following is a list of the principal German documents published in *Nederland in Oorlogstijd* which was furnished to the War Documentation Project by the Netherlands State Institute for War-Documentation.

Issue of
1947

P. 88
Letter of Dr. W. Harster, Befehlshaber der Sicherheitspolizei und des SD, The Hague, to the Reichskommisar, Dr. A. Seyss-Inquart, on transport of Jews to the internment camp of Theresienstadt, 19 August 1943.

P. 102
Protocol of A. A. Mussert, leader of the Nationaal-Socialistische Beweging der Nederlanden, swearing loyalty to Hitler, 12 December 1941.

P. 126
Last order of the day issued by General Blaskowitz, German Commander-in-Chief in the Netherlands, 5 May 1945.

P. 177
First page of the first report on conditions in the occupied Netherlands drawn up for Hitler by Dr. A. Seyss-Inquart, 19 July 1940.

1948
P. 32
Telegram from H. A. Rauter, Hoeherer SS—und Polizeifuehrer, The Hague, to Reichsfuehrer SS Himmler on mass strikes in the Netherlands, 29 April 1943.

P. 33
Telexreport of the Reichsfuehrer SS Himmler to H. A. Rauter, Hoeherer SS—und Polizeifuehrer,

The Hague, congratulating him on the suppression
of the strikes in Holland, 9 May 1943.

P. 39

Telereport of H. A. Rauter, Hoeherer SS—und
Polizeifuehrer, The Hague, to Reichsfuehrer SS Himm-
ler, expressing gratitude for his congratulations, 12
May 1943.

P. 64

First page of a report from K. Daluego, Chef der
Ordnungspolizei, Berlin, on the conference on conditions in occupied European countries, held under the presidency of Goering, 7 August 1942.

P. 68–69

Two pages of a telereport from Befehlshaber
Friedrichs of the Parteikanzlei der NSDAP to
Reichsleiter Martin Bormann on the suicide of
Generalkommissar F. Schmidt, The Hague, 26 June
1943.

P. 92–93

Two telegrams of the German ex-Crown Prince
Wilhelm to Hitler, congratulating him on his vic-
tories, 6 May 1940 and 25 June 1940.
A telegram of the German ex-Emperor Wilhelm
II to Hitler, congratulating him on his victory in
western Europe, 17 June 1940.
A telegram from Hitler to ex-Emperor Wilhelm
II, expressing gratitude for his congratulations, 25 June
1940.

1949

P. 7

First page of a letter from H. A. Rauter, Hoeherer SS—und Polizeifuehrer, The Hague, to the
Reichsfuehrer SS Himmler reporting on the deportation of Dutch Jews, 24 September 1942.

1950

P. 5

First page of a report of H. A. Rauter, Hoeherer
SS—und Polizeifuehrer, The Hague, to the German
military commander in the Netherlands on the strike
movement in Amsterdam 25 and 26 February 1941, 4
March 1941.

P. 5

Fourth page of the same report.

Revue d'Histoire de la Deuxième Guerre Mondiale

(Comité d'Histoire de la Guerre, Société
de l'Histoire de la Guerre, Centre National
de la Recherche Scientifique, Paris)

1 (1951), No. 4, 19-32.

Élisabeth Dunan, "La *Propaganda-Abteilung* de France: Tâches et Organisation."

An article based on and concerning documents of the German propaganda service in
France during the occupation. The following
collections were found:

1. Propaganda-Abteilung Frankreich and
   Propaganda - Abteilung Frankreich,
   Propaganda-Staffel Paris
   Some files of these offices were found in
   Paris, they are now apparently kept
   in the Archives départementales du
   Cher and in the Archives Nationales.

2. Propaganda - Abteilung Frankreich,
   Aussenstelle Bourges
   Almost complete files found in Bourges

and now kept there in the Archives
départementales.

3. Propaganda - Abteilung Frankreich,
   Aussenstellen.
   Certain minor files of other Aussenstel-
   len are in departmental archives in
   Bourg, Lille and Tours.

Sonntagsblatt (Hamburg), September, 1951.

"Was wir noch schwarz auf weiss besit-
zen."

A brief discussion of the Deutsche
Zentralarchiv of the Deutsche Demokra-
tische Republik (Soviet Zone) in Potsdam.
Contains remnants of the Reichsarchiv, the
Preussische Geheime Staatsarchiv, and the
Brandenburgisch-Preussische Hausarchiv.
Also has other files of former eastern sec-
tions of Germany (now under Russian or
Polish rule).

Die Welt als Geschichte (Stuttgart)

Vol. 11 (1951), 122-33.

Gordon A. Craig, "Briefe Schleichers an
Groener." The full texts of all letters from
Schleicher to Groener in the years 1929-
1934 in the Groener Papers in the U.S. National Archives.

Wiener Library Bulletin

Wiener Library, 19 Manchester Square, London, W. 1

In the Periodicals Room of the Library of
Congress, no catalog number, the following volumes are available:

Volume I   Nos 1-6   Nov 1946—Sept 1947
Volume II Nos 1-6   Nov 1947—Sept 1948
Volume III Nos 1-6   Jan 1949—Nov 1949
Volume IV Nos 1-6   Jan 1950—Nov 1950
Volume V   Nos 1-2   Jan 1951—Mar 1951

Vol. 1 (1946), 8

Wiener Library has available "special collections of documents submitted by a number of governments, France, Poland, Yugoslavia and Czechoslovakia, otherwise unpublished."

Vol. 1 (1946-47), No. 5, p. 22

Wiener Library has "Budget of the Reichskommissar Ostland," Riga, 1942, stenciled.
Also, some confidential publications of the
Deutsche Auslands-Institut at Stuttgart
and the Nazi Foreign Organization at Hamburg, dated 1942-1944, including a special set
of publications marked "For Official Use
Only", being extracts from foreign publications translated into German and some statistical handbooks on Germans in foreign
countries. The stenciled reports of the
Fichte-Bund for 1941 are at the Wiener Li-

brary. Also at the Wiener Library is a memorandum, marked "Strictly Confidential" and "Not for Publication," issued by the Institute for Labor Research of the German Labor Front (Deutsche Arbeitsfront, DAF), Berlin, 1940, under the title of "The Social Structure and Economic Position of the Volk Germans from Eastern Europe." Another publication at the Wiener Library is entitled "Bevoelkerungsstatistik des litauischen Staates mit besonderer Beruecksichtigung der Deutschen," Berlin, 1935, published by the Publikationsstelle Berlin-Dahlem (Supplement, Berlin, 1940).

Vol. 2 (1948), 20

"Geheim" volume from Reichsfuehrer SS H. Himmler with biographies of German opponents of National Socialism (stenciled): "Erfassung Fuehrender Maenner der Sy-stemzeit." June 1939; numbered copies. The Wiener Library has copy No. 13.

Vol. 3 (1949), 15

Article on the "Central Historical Commission" attached to the Central Committee of Liberated Jews in the United States Zone, now ending its activities. Its task and materials have been transferred to the "Yad va'Shem". In addition to the vast archive from Dachau, the Commission possesses nearly 2,000 assorted documents of Jewish as well as Nazi origin, relating to life under the Nazis. They have also films: five depicting German entry into Poland, and an anti-Semitic hate film. Twenty-eight thousand Nazi documents filmed, mainly concerned with looted Jewish property. Also have most of the archives of the Jewish community of Franconia (the Franken district of Bavaria) dating back to the 17th century.

PART III

Depositories

Depositories

THE MATERIAL in the following lists is not classified. The listings have, to a very large extent, been prepared by members of the staff of the War Documentation Project. Some of the identifications are still tentative and it is hoped that researchers making use of the materials will give additional information on them to the War Documentation Project as well as to the depository in which the material is located.

Anyone interested in using the documents listed here, or in securing photostats or microfilms, should communicate directly with the depository, not with the War Documentation Project.

Chapter 1

CENTRE DE DOCUMENTATION JUIVE
CONTEMPORAINE, PARIS

ASIDE from an extensive collection of material from the Nuremberg Trials, the Centre has holdings of the following groups of German documents:

1. The Rosenberg files. A collection of documents from the files of Alfred Rosenberg; including material from the NSDAP, Institut zur Erforschung der Judenfrage; Reichsministerium fuer die besetzten Ostgebiete; and Beauftragter des Fuehrers fuer die Ueberwachung der gesamten geistigen und weltanschaulichen Erziehung der NSDAP.

2. Reichssicherheitshauptamt (RSHA). A group of 800 documents.

3. Auswaertiges Amt. A group of documents from the German legation in Hungary (papers of Veesenmayer).

4. Auswaertiges Amt, Deutsche Botschaft Paris. A group of about 200 documents from the German Embassy in Paris, including papers of Counselor C. T. Zeitschel.

5. Gestapo. Documents from the office of the Gestapo in France.

6. Militaerbefehlshaber Frankreich. Documents from the office of the Militaerbefehlshaber Frankreich.

The Centre sponsors the publication *Le Monde Juif* (see under Part II) in which the texts of some of its documents have been published.

The Centre is also the sponsor of a number of books and monographs. Those containing captured documents are included in Part I of this bibliography (Éditions du Centre).

NOTE: For additional information on the character, organization, and indexing of the archives of the Centre, see Centre de Documentation Juive Contemporaine, *Sur les Chantiers de Nos Archives* (Paris, 1951), 15 pp.

Chapter 3

HOOVER INSTITUTE AND LIBRARY

THE HOOVER INSTITUTE collection of German materials consists of the units listed below. (It is strongly recommended that in each case inquiry be made in advance whether or not the materials are sufficiently processed and thus available for historical research):

1. The Himmler files

Reichsfuehrer SS. Persoenlicher Stab, Schriftgutverwaltung. Parts of the Himmler files on photostat, organised according to the original system of the Persoenliche Stab. Detailed information on these files will be found in Appendix 1. It should be noted that the subject index to the Himmler files in the Hoover Library refers only to specific items of interest and was prepared by the Hoover Library staff. The list of Himmler files in the Library of Congress, Manuscripts Division, (q. v.), refers to the general subject matter of each folder and was prepared by the WDP.

2. N.S.D.A.P. Gauleitung Berlin.
See Appendix 2.

3. Adjutantur des Fuehrers.
Documents from the Adjutantur des Fuehrers. See Appendix 3.

4. Anti-Komintern Collection.
A collection of materials from the Anti-Komintern files and from Anti-Komintern, Abteilung: Sowjetunion. See Appendix 4.

5. Reichskanzlei.
Folders from the Reichskanzlei. See Appendix 5.

6. Fuehrer und Reichskanzler.
See Appendix 6.

7. Tannenbergbund and Folkish movement in general.
See Appendix 7.

8. Various items from German agencies.
NSDAP, US.
Auswaertiges Amt.
IG Farben.
NSDAP, Reichsorganisationsleiter.
NSDAP, Fluechtlingsfuersorge.
Einsatzstab Reichsleiter Rosenberg (Auszuege aus dem Mitteilungsblatt).
Deutsche Kongress-Zentrale.
Reichssicherheitsdienst.
Kommandeur von Gross-Paris.
See Appendix 8.

The Hoover Institute also has materials of the following agencies:

NSDAP, Deutsche Arbeitsfront, 1939-40;
Nationalsozialistischer Dozentenbund, 1935-36;
Sonderdienst Seehaus.

9. Materials of biographical character.
Diary and papers of Josef Goebbels (see Appendix 9). Papers of Wilfrid Bade, an official of the Reichsministerium fuer Volksaufklaerung und Propaganda.

NOTE: On the holdings of the Hoover Institute, see also: Van der Belen, Jacques, *Inventaire de la collection consacrée à "La Belgique dans la Deuxième Guerre Mondiale" réunie par les soins de la Belgian American Educational Foundation, Inc., à l'intention de la Hoover Library, Stanford University, California.* Brussels: Les Presses Tilbury, 1950. 128 pp. Official and private documents cataloged.

Certain captured German documents formerly held by the Psychological Warfare Division of SHAEF are now at the Hoover Institute. For information on these, see in Part I under Lerner, Daniel, *Sykewar.*

Appendix 1

Hoover Library Himmler Files

Explanatory Note to the Himmler Files

The material was organized in the Hoover Library in 18 pamphlet boxes numbered I to XVIII. The label attached to each box indicates the folder numbers of the material contained therein. The boxes are stored in the vault.

Attached to this note is a listing of the contents of each of the 18 boxes, according to drawer number, "Mappe" number, and folder number.

Also attached to this note is a "Preliminary Subject Index to Himmler Files" which lists only the more important material contained in the files.

Himmler Files — Contents of Boxes

Box No.	Drawer No.	Mappe No.	Folder No.
I.	10	N 349	51- 53
II.	10	N 350	55- 69
III.	10	N 350	70
IV.	7	N 335	251-261
V.	7	N 335	262-264
	7	N 336	265
VI.	7	N 336	266, 268-273
	? (7)	?	274-275
VII.	? (7)	?	276-281
VIII.	? (7)	?	282-285
	7	N 336	286-288
IX.	7	N 338	289-290
X.	7	N 339	291-300
XI.	8	N 340	301-309
XII.	8	N 341	310-315
XIII.	8	N 341	316-318
	8	N 342	319
XIV.	8	N 342	320-326
XV.	8	N 343	327-332
XVI.	8	N 344	333-337
	8	N 344	339-344
XVII.	9	?	351-356
XVIII.	9	?	357-362
			365,370

Preliminary Subject Index to Himmler Files

This index lists only the more important material contained in the Himmler Files.

Folder   Subject
No.

of all armed forces of Germany (Hitler's orders of July 20 and August 2, 1944).

358 Folder, Johann (Hans) Loritz (Commander of K. Z. Dachau and Sachsenhausen).

360 Folder, Paul Oertel ("Aktion Wieland"); cf. Folder No. 290.

367 Concerning the Rumanian "Iron Guard" Refugees in Germany (Sturdza and others).

365 Concerning the internal organization of the SS.

370 Concerning General Bor (Komorowski) in war prisoner camp in Germany.

Appendix 2
Hoover Library

Explanatory Note and Inventory of Collection of Files

Germany — NSDAP, Gauleitung Berlin

This collection consists of five folders of miscellaneous material, which was organized in the following manner:

1. *Files of the Office of "Der Mobilisationsbeauftragte" (Petzold)* in the Berlin Gauleitung; the files cover the period 1938-1941 and are quite complete. They contain a probably complete collection of secret circulars and ordinances of the Chief of the Mobilization Office (Division "M") of the NSDAP under Rudolf Hess' leadership. The files in this collection are in two folders marked "Part II."

2. *Files of the Stennes case* contain a copious documentation of the defection in the Berlin SA in 1931 under the leadership of Captain Stennes, and the purge in the NSDAP which followed the incident.

3. The folder *Gau-Organisationsamt Berlin, Hauptstelle Statistik: Rulings for statistics of the NSDAP of July 1, 1939* contains a complete collection of ordinances concerning the party census in 1939 (Parteistatistische Erhebung).

4. The folder *Miscellaneous* contains scattered files of various offices in the Berlin Gauleitung for the period 1939-1941.

Appendix 3
Hoover Library

Explanatory Note and Inventory of the Collection of Files from the *Adjutantur des Fuehrers*.

The files cover the period 1933 - 1938, but most of them are from the years 1934 - 1936. The collection is made up of original files and is organized in the following folders:

1. Wiedemann's Miscellaneous Files (three folders).

2. Gestapo Case Dr. Georg Banasch (1935).

3. Miscellanea concerning Austria (1936).

4. The Italo-Ethiopian War, 1936 (Strunk von Este).

5. The Hamburg subway.

6. Mail Record (May-August, 1940).

7. Folder Darré.

Appendix 4
Anti-Komintern Collection

1. Liste grundlegender kommunistischer und prokommunistischer Gesellschaften und Organisationen ausserhalb der Sowjetunion.
   Ausweichstelle Freyburg/Unstrut, dated 29 Nov. 1944.
   (Group 41/8.)

2. Letter of Alex. von Melgunoff to Dr. Goebbels, dated Aug. 11, 1941, offering his services. (Group 41/26a.)

3. Alex. von Melgunoff "Die deutsche Sendung .m Osten" (dated March 1944); against the authenticity of the so-called last will of Peter the Great. (Group 41/7.)

4. Estnische Verwaltung.
   Stalin geht zum Angriff ueber.
   Leidensjahr des estnischen Volkes. 25 pp.

5. Materialien ueber die Schreckensherrschaft der Bolschewisten in Estland.
   1940-41. Dated 20 Oct. 1943. 29 pp.

6. Amt fuer Estland.
   Bolschewistische Wirtschaft in Estland, 1940-41. Dated Oct. 1941. 46 pp.

7. Die Ukrainer und der Bolschewismus.
   Undated. 36 pp.

8. Die Ukrainer und der Bolschewismus.
   April 1944. 36 pp.

9. Aufbau des Volkskommissariates fuer innere Angelegenheiten der SU.
   (NKVD) 1941. 24 pp. Nine photo-copies.

10. Clipping archives arranged according to countries.

11. Institut zum Studium der Judenfrage.
    Several folders.

12. Sonderdienst der NS Presse.
    Several folders.

13. Radio Propaganda in Russian.
    (Broadcast in October 1944 of the Voennyi sojuz natsionalistov russkago naroda.)

14. Aufklaerung und Reden und Informationsmaterial der Reichspropagandaleitung der NSDAP und des Reichspropagandaamtes der Deutschen Arbeitsfront, Lieferung 4/5 (April-Mai 1944): Bolschewismus. (Zentralverlag der NSDAP.)

15. Carlo von Kuegelgen: Die Entwicklung in Finnland nach Abschluss des Waffenstillstandsvertrages, 19 Sept. 1944. Dated Oct. 1944. 10 pp.

16. Reichssicherheitshauptamt
Stellungnahme zur "Zusammenfassung ueber die Personal-und Materiallage der sowjet-russischen Wehrmacht Anfang Juni 1944." 5 Okt. 1944. 7 pp.

Anti-Komintern, Abteilung: Sowjetunion

1. Die kommunistische Infiltration in Skandinavien. Materialzusammenstellung aus der Sowjetpresse. (Group 37/18.) Dated July 7, 1944. 13 pp.

2. Die Behandlung internationaler Vertraege durch die Bolschewisten. (Group 37/18.) Dated 15 July 1944.

3. Die Russischen Emigranten in Serbien und der Bolschewismus. No date. 8 pp.

4. Mergenthaler: "Ungarn und der Bolschewismus." 2 Parts, 43 and 29 pages. No date.

5. Das Problem der ukrainischen und weissrussischen Staatenlosen.

6. Allgemeine Bemerkungen zur Tabelle des Staatshaushaltes der UdSSR in den Jahren 1918-1944. Dated May 12, 1944. Text and statistics.

7. Mich. Antonowitsch: "Das Schicksal der ukrainischen Gelehrten in der Sowjet-Ukraine." (Group 11a/3.) No date. 3 pp.

8. UHWR (Ukrainska Holowna Wyzwolna Rada): Ukrainischer Hauptbefreiungsrat. General policy statement (Universal) of June 15, 1944. 10 pp.

Appendix 5

Reichskanzlei
Several folders on the German budget, 1878-1936.
Folder with financial regulations during the Second World War.
Folder on Verwaltungsakademien, 1933.
Staatsbegraebnis (State funeral) des Gesandtschaftsrates Pg. vom Rath, 16-17, November 1938.

Appendix 6

Fuehrer und Reichskanzler
Fuehrerschutzkommando
Tagebuch (letter reception book), 1934-35.
Begleitkommando des Fuehrers.
Tagebuch (letter reception book), 1943-44.

Appendix 7
Tannenbergbund
Nachrichtenblatt, 1932-33.
Verordnungsblatt des Gau Berlin, 1931-33.

Printed materials on German Freemasonry; membership lists of lodges.
Ludendorff materials and correspondence of Ludendorff with adherents of the folkish movement.
Miscellaneous materials of the folkish movement.

Appendix 8
NSDAP: SS
Ehrenhaendel: SS-Hauptfuehrer Roland Strunk und Obergebietsfuehrer Horst Krutschinna, 1937.

Auswaertiges Amt
Diewerge, *Der Fall Gustloff* (geheim), 19. Oktober, 1936. Sachbericht im Mordprozess gegen den Juden David Frankfurter [Attentat gegen den Landesgruppenleiter Schweiz der NSDAP, Wilhelm Gustloff, am 4. Feb. 1936.]
Letter dated Oct. 1936 from Abteilungsleiter VII (gez. v. Feldmann) an Staatssekretaer (v. Weizsaecker.)

Bruno Luxenberg
Denkschriften ueber die Versorgungslage Deutschlands.

IG Farben
Rundschreiben der Propagandaabteilung.

NSDAP, Reichsorganisationsleiter
Correspondence: 1936-37.

NSDAP, Fluechtlingsfuersorge
Correspondence: West evacuation 1939-40.
Auszuege aus dem Mitteilungsblatt des Einsatzstabes Rosenberg:
Teil 1. Wie sieht und beurteilt die Sowjetbevoelkerung den Bolschewismus. 4 pp.
Deutsche Kongress-Zentrale (under supervision of Reichsministerium fuer Volksaufklaerung und Propaganda):
Materials on organizations and conventions in the whole world, including printed materials.

Reichssicherheitsdienst
Material for the training of Gestapo men.
Kommandeur von Gross-Paris, Kommando Stab:
Kommando-Befehle No. 115 (Nov. 19, 1940), to No. 179 (Dec. 3, 1941).
Reichssicherheitshauptamt
Geheime Staatspolizei (Amt IV)

1. Printed list of persons to be arrested in England after invasion (1940).

2. Informationsheft Grossbritannien (1940?). 376 p.

Appendix 9

The diary and papers of Josef Goebbels.
The original manuscript of the Goebbels

diary for the following dates is on deposit with the Hoover Institute:

   August 12, 1925 - October 16, 1926,
   January 21 - May 23, 1942 (March 22-25 and April 10 missing),
   December 7 - 20, 1942,
   March 1 - 20, 1943,
   April 9-May 28, 1943 (May 26 missing),
   July 25 - 30, 1943,
   November 1 - 30, 1943 (November 5 and 28 missing),

December 4 - 9, 1943.

(See Joseph Goebbels, *The Goebbels Diaries 1942-1943*. L. P. Lochner ed., pp. 3, 5-11.)

Papers of Joseph Goebbels:

   Deposited with the Hoover Institute is a small group of personal papers, dated approximately 1931-1945. For a listing of some of the items in the group, see Joseph Goebbels, *The Goebbels Diaries*, 1942-1943, pp. vi-viii.

THE LIBRARY OF CONGRESS

THE HOLDINGS of captured German materials deposited in the Library of Congress are very extensive. They are therefore listed in separate sections according to custodial division. Regulations and procedures for access to the materials should be obtained from the division under which they are listed.

Section I	Quarterly Journal of Current Acquisitions (This periodical is published by the Library of Congress and gives information concerning its holdings)
Section II.	Captured German materials accessioned into the main collection of the Library of Congress.
Section III.	The Film Division.
Section IV.	Map Division.
Section V.	Microfilm Section.
Section VI.	Aëronautics Division.
Section VII.	Rare Books Division.
Section VIII.	Prints and Photographs Division.
Section IX.	Music Division.
Section X.	Newspaper Division: Materials placed on deposit with the Government Documents Section of the LC by the U. S. Department of Commerce and serviced by the Newspaper Division.
Section XI.	Manuscripts Division.
Section XII.	Exchange and Gift Division.

Section I

Library of Congress: *Quarterly Journal of Current Acquisitions*: (Z 881 U5, Q3)

Vol. 3 (1945–46), No. 4, pp. 7-9.

Lederer, Max. "The Deutsche Auslands-Institut." On the transfer of its archives to the Library of Congress after seizure by the United States Army in Stuttgart. Includes bibliographies and documents of Nazi Party, including "confidential" and "secret" circulars; Party publications for "internal use only." See Manuscripts Division, Appendix 1.

Vol. 3 (1945-46), No. 4, pp. 41-42.

Eells, Richard. "Aëronautical Science." Captured German air documents will go eventually to the Library of Congress after processing at Wright Field, Dayton, Ohio; include 220 tons of documents. Other air documents coming through the CIOS (Combined Intelligence Objectives Subcommittee), BIOS (British Intelligence Objectives Subcommittee), and FIAT (Field Information Agency, Technical), and also the Himmler Files.

Vol. 4 (1946-47), No. 1, p. 44.

Library of Congress received 26,384 reels of impounded or captured German films through the War Department: war training films, newsreels, general documentaries, photoplays.

Vol. 4 (1946-47), No. 4, pp. 27-28.

Library of Congress to be final depository of all captured, declassified aëronautical literature received from FIAT and Wright Field.

Vol. 4 (1946-47), No. 4, pp. 28-31.

Confiscated libraries in the Library of Congress. The Aëronautics Division of the Library of Congress has received sections of the libraries of the following:
Junkers and Focke-Wulf factories,
Deutsche Akademie fuer Luftfahrtforschung.
Deutsche Forschungsanstalt fuer Segelflug,
Reichsluftfahrtministerium.

Vol. 4 (1946-47), No. 4, p. 60.

"Several thousand German reproductions of Russian and Norwegian charts" transferred to Map Division, Library of Congress.

Vol. 4 (1946-47), No. 4, p. 63.

Further details on air materials transferred, or to be transferred, to the Library of Congress via CIOS, BIOS, and FIAT.

Vol. 5 (1947-48), No. 2, p. 20.

The Library of Congress has received some more captured German films from the Department of the Army.

Vol. 5 (1947-48), No. 4, pp. 21-22.

Aëronautics article, by R. Eells and staff, further discussion of the Wright Field documents.

Vol. 6 (1948-49), No. 1, pp. 21-22.

Stuurman, Douwe. "The Nazi Collection," concerns the activities of the Library of Congress Mission to Germany. The article was a preview of what was to be sent to the library. According to Mr. Obear, of the Library of Congress staff, most of the documents listed in this article failed to reach the Library of Congress; they have not been located yet. The documents include:

Nazi Party Archives
Police Records
Party Materials
Newspapers
Chancellery Records
Master recordings of Nazi speeches (Cf. Section IX).

Vol. 6 (1948-49), No. 1, pp. 88-89.

(a) Library of Congress has acquired an extensive collection of prints and photographs containing Hermann Goering's collection, 1933-1942.

(b) Photo reports of the Daimler-Benz auto firm, 48 albums of 1940.

(c) 75,000 negatives from the files of a free-lance photographer of Stuttgart, Wolf Strache.

For more details, see under holdings of the Prints and Photographs Division of the Library of Congress.

Vol. 6 (1948-49), No. 4, pp. 21-27.

Vanderbilt, Paul. "Prints and Photographs of Nazi Origin."

A survey of many thousands of pictures captured in Germany and now in the Prints and Photographs Division of the Library of Congress—each lot entered and described on one card.

For more details, see under holdings of the Prints and Photographs Division of the Library of Congress.

Vol. 6 (1948-49), No. 4, pp. 44-49.

Library of Congress gets the von Rohden Collection. The collection consists mainly of German Air Force and other German official records. In addition, there are manuscripts of members of the von Rohden project after the war on the history of the air war. Part of the original collection is in London and part at Maxwell Field. For further information see under the Aëronautics Division of the Library of Congress.

Section II—Main Collection

Sections of certain captured libraries have been accessioned directly into the main library holdings and can be located through the main catalog. These include books selected from the libraries of Gerdy Troost, Frank, Himmler, and possibly Goebbels. Some parts of the Bibliothek (des Instituts?) zur Erforschung der Judenfrage have been accessioned, one item is in the Manuscripts Division. Books supplementing Library of Congress holdings from the library of Wehrkreiskommando XII have been accessioned; a list exists of the material originally in this library.

In addition, a large number of individual captured German items, classified by the Germans, have been accessioned into the main collection. These can be located only through the card catalog, particularly under the names of various German government agencies and military offices and units. For publications of various German government agencies concerning the occupied eastern territories between 1941 and 1945 look under the following entries:

1. Germany, Reichsministerium des Innern, Publikationsstelle Berlin-Dahlem; also Publikationsstelle Ost.

2. Reichsministerium fuer die besetzten Ostgebiete.

Section III—Film Division

(Care of Mr. James H. Culver, Custodian of the Motion Picture Collection, in the microfilm reading room.)

The library's holdings can be divided into the following four groups:

1. Enemy alien films impounded by the United States at the outbreak of war. Under control of Alien Property Custodian.

2. German feature films, cultural subjects, amusement films, newsreels, and similar material.

3. German military training films, 35 mm. There is a great deal of duplication. This is the only part of an immense collection on which indexing work has been done. A listing is in the library.

4. About 100 cases of unopened 16 mm film.

See also Section I.

Section IV—Map Division

Germany, Beauftragter fuer den Vierjahresplan.

"Goering's Atlas." Berlin, 1946. 83 colored maps. Maps outlining the raw material resources and industrial plants of primary importance to German war efforts, prepared by the Office of the Delegate for the Four Year Plan in the spring of 1944 on the basis of information for 1942 and 1943. The maps were put together in their present form by the American occupation authorities.

See also Section I.

Section V—Microfilm Section

There is no separate listing or guide to show what captured German material is here. A search of the card catalog under "Germany" revealed one film: No. 1223. Aside from clippings about July 20, 1944 and anti-Nazi pamphlets and letters, it contains a copy of a paper entitled:

"Abteilung fuer Militaerpolitik," September 1937. This seems to be a military intelligence report on a branch of the German Communist Party (KPD) of the above name. Mainly Weimar period.

The Microfilm Section has a six-reel microfilm copy of the Goebbels Diary for 1942-1943 in the Hoover Institute and Library.

Section VI—Aeronautics Division

The holdings can be divided into three parts:

1. The von Rohden collection.

   The originals of the von Rohden collection are partly in London and partly at Maxwell Air Force Base. The Aeronautics Division has a large part of the total collection on microfilm. The material covers all aspects of the Second World War and includes diplomatic as well as purely military and political material. An inventory of the LC microfilms which gives an inventory number and a very brief description of each item is kept in the office of Mr. Marvin W. McFarland, consultant to the chief of the Division.

2. Books and periodicals.

   A considerable number of books and a large number of periodicals, largely for the war years, are in the stacks of the Aeronautics Division.

3. Unprocessed documents and materials from Wright Field. This is a very large mass of material, most of it of a technical nature and including some books. A part of the technical material is organized by type of plane, like Messerschmidt. There are intelligence reports on planes of various countries. All the important Allies are included. There are also:

   Reichsluftfahrtministerium, statistical files.

   Reichswehrministerium, Heereswaffenamt, 1933, three folders.

   Reichswehrministerium, Inspektion der Waffenschulen, 1927-1931, five folders.

   Preussen, Kriegsministerium, General-Inspektion des Militaer-Verkehrswesens, 1912-1918.

   Bayern, Staatsministerium des Aeussern, air matters, 1932-1934, three folders.

   Regierung Niederbayern, Kammer des Innern, Verkehr mit Luftfahrzeugen, 1912-1932.

   Bayern, Luftverein, two folders.

   Bayern, Akt der Koenigl. Inspektion des Militaer-Luftfahrwesens, 1917-1918.

   Bayern, Koenigliche Inspektion des Ingenieurkorps, 1915-1916.

   Propaganda pictures including captured Russian pictures.

   One folder of correspondence of the RLM with the Deutsche Waffenstillstandskommission in Wiesbaden

concerning demands to be made on the French, 1940-1941.

Some envelopes of material, including Russian request for material from Germany, 1939-1940.

"Bericht ueber den Besuch der russischen Luftfahrtkommission bei den Lizenzwerken des Motorenbaues, 12 Jan. 1940."

See also Section I.

Section VII—Rare Books Division

The Rare Books Division has the following materials, mostly in unprocessed and uncataloged form. The material is, however, shelved.

1. Hitler Library (in two parts, one called the Reichskanzlei library). Several hundred books, folios, and photograph albums from the Hitler library. Many books on art and architecture, mostly complimentary copies, the rest on a variety of current topics. Cataloging of these books has been started.

2. Eva Braun Library. Most of these books, which supposedly belonged to Eva Braun, are ascribed to her by mistake, as evidenced by various library stamps in them.

3. Literature, photographs, and photostats dedicated to Hitler.

4. Fine bindings and other items such as folios and a book register from the library of Hermann Goering.

5. Some folios entitled *Fuehrerankaeufe*, apparently pictures and other items purchased for Hitler.

6. A number of special books, presentation volumes etc. from the Constantin von Neurath Collection.

7. A collection of posters, leaflets etc. from the Rehse-Archiv (Hauptarchiv der NSDAP).

8. There are a few miscellaneous items, including a presentation volume from the library of Heinrich Himmler.

9. Included with the Hitler library, but possibly not a part of it, is a set of "Die Alte Garde spricht." - a series of typed autobiographies of Nazi Party members, organized by Gau and bound into several volumes.

10. Small groups from the libraries of Streicher, Frank, Schwartz, Strasser.

Section VIII—Prints and Photographs Division

The Prints and Photographs Division has a very large number of items captured in Germany such as

Parts of the Rehse collection.

Photograph collection of Hermann Goering.

Items from the Deutsche Arbeitsfront.

Photographs and pictures of and about the Hitler Youth, army, air force, Kraft durch Freude, NSDAP Volkswohlfahrt, etc.

All items or groups of items have been given numbers and cards for each number made and entered into a subject catalog (see under Germany) and a numerical catalog. The German materials are scattered through the numerical sequence.

A very useful guide is being published: "Selective Checklist of Prints and Photographs recently cataloged and made available for reference."

Three issues have appeared, Lots 2280-2984, 2985-3442, and 3443-4120. A fourth issue is in preparation. The highest number of a captured German lot in the numerical catalog is now No. 5774, but most of the important material will have been covered when the next issue appears. The cards in the division give slightly more complete information about each lot than the checklist. See also Section I.

The following excerpts from some of the lot numbers listed in the checklists of the Prints and Photographs Division will illustrate the nature of the holdings of this division. The items selected for this list have been chosen because of their importance, origin, or representative character. This is *not* a complete list. All lots are referred to and cataloged by number, and more information about each lot can be obtained from the card catalog of the division.

2347. Heidelberg, Germany. 1936-39 (?). Unique album on activities of a Nazi training school, under the title: *Langemarck-Studium der Reichsstudentenfuehrung, Lehrgang Heidelberg.*

2369. German military railroad construction in Russia. Oct. 1943. Seventy-one indistinct progress photos.

2429. Activities of the Nationalsozialistische Volkswohlfahrt ("NSV"), the welfare organization of the Nazi party in Germany. 1940-45 (?). (Approx. 100 photos.)

2439. Anti-Hitler color posters; some photographs and some cartoons. Six crude prints. From the Rehse collection.

2498. Calendar of portrait photographs of leading Nazi officials. Biographical summary captions. From the Haupt-Archiv der NSDAP, Munich.

2500. A selection of German propaganda illustrated wall-newspapers, mainly in Russian and Polish, a few in languages of other occupied areas, 1941. War combat and "home front" subject matter. Current news, developments in Germany, destruction, atrocities, peaceful peasant occupations, cheering reception of German troops, German

personalities, etc. Series title: *Aktualne ilustracje, Nova vasi,* etc. Forty sheets.

2627. Daimler-Benz, A. G. Firm, automobile mfgrs. Germany. Leistungsbericht, 1940. Exhaustive photo-report on all aspects of the company's activity, handsomely mounted in albums. Forty-three vols. of set of 53.

2651. *Grossdeutschland im Weltgeschehen.* Albums of German photographs depicting the progress of the war at the battle fronts and at home, 1939-42. Approx. 750 photos publ. by Reichsministerium fuer Volksaufklaerung und Propaganda.

2652. Stettin, Germany. 1936. *Stosstrupp Adolf Hitler 1923 in Stettin.* Album of photographs showing the celebration at Stettin of the 12th anniversary of the formation in 1923 of the "shock troops." Approx. 60 photos.

2656. Photographs of Nazi propaganda activities in Saar territory, 1934. Twenty-three photos.

2659. German women in industry, arts, professions and sports, 1941 (?). Photos from the Reichsstudentenfuehrung, Amt Studentinnen.

2669. Adolf Hitler Schule, 1934 (?). Approx. 25 photos.

2670. Muehldorf and vicinity, Germany. 1933-39. *Sieben Jahre Kreis Muehldorf.* Photographic report on the first seven years of Nazism in Muehldorf. Approx. 300 photos issued by Amt fuer Gemeindepolitik. (?) (NSDAP, Hauptamt fuer Kommunalpolitik ?)

2674. *Volksdeutsche Mittelstelle.* A set of photographs of a striking exhibition (1939?) of the Nazi program of repatriation of Germans from southern and south-eastern Europe. Plans for re-settlement, the Nazi conception of the superior type settler, their occupations, etc., the removal of undesirable racial elements. Forty photos of pictorial maps and charts in elaborate portfolio.

2680. Vienna, Austria. Oct. 1938. Album of photos of some of the propaganda activities of the Nationalsozialistischer Lehrerbund (NSLB), German educators' organisation. Approx. 100 photos.

2698. Riga and vicinity, 1942. Photographs of the city and interpretative studies of its people. Captions attempt to prove that its inhabitants were largely German and therefore should be within the German sphere. Incomplete set of 25 photos.

2708. German army engineers sinking wells in Scutari, Valona, and Durazzo, Albania. 1944. Nineteen damaged snapshots in album marked secret; official German Army document. Heeresgruppe F, Kommandeur der Technischen Truppen.

2720. Album of photographs of a German exhibition, 1934, designed to awaken a nationalistic feeling in the farmer, and to mold farm life into the Nazi pattern. Seventy-five photo-copies of posters, photos, graphs, statistical maps, models, etc.

2732. Burgenland, Austria. 1938. *Burgenland, Marsch ins Dritte Reich.* Album of photographs on the annexation of the easternmost province of Austria by Nazi Germany. Thirty-three photos.

2744. Normandy and Brittany, France. Feb. 1944. Album of photographs of the "Atlantic Wall." Approx. 250 snapshot photos.

2755. Album of photographs, 1936, of the German maternity convalescent home, Steinhoering, Bavaria (?), operated by the Verein Lebensborn. Approx. 35 photos.

2761. Hermann Goering, flyer in the first World War, 1918 (?). Nineteen photos.

2766. Collection of photographs of Nazi party training schools and barracks, about 1940. Thirty-two photos.

2784. Album of photographs of Germans in Poland, 1939(?) German guards, Polish soldiers who surrendered for their "self-protection." German efforts at re-settlement of Germans in Poland, deportation of other groups. Russian Repatriation Commission in Lublin. Forty-five snapshots.

2808. *Unser Oberschlesien.* 1935 (?). Sixteen photos, issued by Heimatverlag Oberschlesien, Gleiwitz.

2888. *Altreligioese Ausdrucksformen des Schwabenlandes.* 1938. Archaeological and architectural details of religious buildings and monuments in Svabia, 6th to 18th century. Attempt to document a religious mythology based on the old "noble" Germanic civilization. Approx. 300 photos in two Albums by SS-Obersturmfuehrer Rueppmann from Das Ahnenerbe, a branch of the SS.

2970. Munich and vicinity. 1936-42. Exhaustive collection of news photographs and snapshots mounted in albums under cover title: *Im Kampf um das Dritte Reich*, concerning activities of Gauleiter Adolf Wagner and Nazi official participation in meetings, military events, etc. Anschluss with Austria, Munich conference, 1938, etc., fully treated. Approx. 7,000 photos in 23 albums.

2997. Positive microfilm of posters and proclamations issued by the Germans in France, 1940-44. Approx. 100 frames.

3050. Deutsche Akademie (Munich, Germany). Collection of photographs, arranged alphabetically by city, of propaganda activities, 1935-40 (?), of the Deutsche Akademie, concerning its efforts to establish German study groups in foreign countries. Approx. 900 photos, mainly snapshots.

3070. Miscellaneous lot of photographs of Hermann Goering, his home, relatives, and activities, 1935-42. Aerial and interior views of Carinhall; portraits, groups, official functions, etc. Approx. 35 photos by various German photo agencies, from the Photo-Archiv General-Feldmarschall Goering, a supplement to the organized official collection. See No. 3128.

3073. Collection of photographs of Paul Ludwig Troost, 1878-1934, Nazi architect. Approx. 75 photos.

3128. Extensive personal collection of photographs of Hermann Goering, Reichsmarschall des Grossdeutschen Reiches, made for his official and personal use. Career to 1942 only. (Aviator, 1914-18, gap to 1933.) Nazi party activities, speeches, inspections. Personal life with family, hunting trips, sporting activities, travels. Meetings with officials; Reichstag; connections with air force and Four-year Plan. Homes at Carinhall and in the mountains. News, formal, and "candid" photographs in great variety, from agencies and individuals. Estimated 18,500 photos in 47 albums chronological sequence.

3145. Deutsche Akademie. Miscellaneous photographs apparently submitted to headquarters as appendices to reports by the outposts of the organization formed to establish German study groups in foreign countries for propaganda purposes. Arranged by city, from all over the world. Estimated 1,000 photos of poor quality.

3154. Bilbao, Spain. 1941. Album of photographs of Hitler Youth school and camp for the indoctrination and training of boys and girls. Approx. 125 snapshots.

3348. Album of photographs under the title *Baltische Oelschiefenwerke*, 1943. Plans for oil refineries in Estonia at Kivioeli, Jewe, Koht's-Jaerve . . . to

be built under the auspices of Germany's Arbeitsfront, Organisation Todt, and the Reichswerke. Approx. 50 photos. Transferred from the U. S. Army War College in 1945.

3414. Backnang (and vicinity). Germany, 1934-35. Small single housing units constructed under the direction of a Nazi-sponsored cooperative building association. Approx. 75 photos.

3430. Collection of albums of photographs dealing with activities of the *German Reichspost*, 1933-45.—Approx. 500 photos, mainly uncaptioned, in 15 albums.

3458. Set of photographs of *German public works*, 1936-40. Approx. 45 mounted, captioned photos.

3534. Students' course work in a Berlin School of *advertising art*, typography and layout, 1931-32.—Approx. 100 items.

3564. German reprints of *Allied cartoons*, about 1940, in which Allied publications are critical of themselves and each other. Approx. 35 unmounted clippings.

3575. Original cartoons by Seppla, one of Germany's leading *Nazi cartoonists*, 1935-45.—Approx. 150 drawings.

3597. Extensive collection of all kinds of *German money and scrip*, 1914-24, chiefly the currency used during and after the first World war, issued by states, German colonial administrations, cities, large corporations, prisoner-of-war camps, and in some cases, individuals. Some Austrian money. One album is devoted to the huge denominations issued during the ruinous inflation, 1919-23 etc. Eighteen albums containing roughly 25,000 items, compiled for the Rehse collection.

3613. Romantic photographs of the rugged German countryside, country villages, picturesque farm homes, cultivated fields, orchards, and vineyards. —Nazi attempt to document an early "noble" *Germanic civilization.* Approx. 150 photos.

3615. Collection of clippings from several German newspapers on the public life of Frankenfuehrer (Franconian leader) *Julius Streicher*, 1924-29. Approx. 125 mounted clippings with date and name of newspaper.

3617. Portrait photographs of *Nazi Senior and Junior officers* of the Wehrmacht, 1939-45. Incomplete set by Heinrich Hoffmann, official photographer of the NSDAP.

3620. Incomplete set of reproductions of photographs of the *early Nazi activities*, 1922-32, in Germany, under running title: Deutschland erwacht.

3641. Early photographs of Adolf Hitler, 1920-1933, and one of him as a child in a classroom photograph.

3643. Several *German construction projects*, chiefly performed by the Arbeitsdienst, the National Labor Service, 1933-40.

3644. Groups of portraits and news photographs, 1930-45, of the activities of prominent *Jews* in several countries: poor unidentified Jews, Talmudic students, etc. Chosen to emphasize the Nazi theory of the corrupt physical, moral, mental, and artistic influence of the Jews, with highly biased captions in German. Approx. 100 photos.

3645. *German women in uniform*, Luftwaffenhelferinnen, 1939-45.

3657. Activities of the Nationalsozialistische Volkswohlfahrt of Germany. Approx. 35 photos.

3658. Extensive collection of photo copies of *German posters* of 1914-33. First World War sheets asking for enlistments and loans; revolutionary posters calling for a general strike in 1918; Nazi

Communist, and Social Democratic election propaganda, etc., etc. Numbered, small photos in albums, accompanied by lists specifying printers, place, and artist. Rehse Collection.

3575. Trials of the men and women involved in the attempt on *Adolf Hitler's* life in July, 1944; Graf von Moltke, Fuerst Fugger von Gloett, Gen. Stuelpnagel standing before the judges; many uniformed police. Approx. 100 news photos, chiefly by Presse-Hoffmann, some captioned on back with defendant's name and in a few cases with note of the sentence imposed.

3715. Book of virulent *Italian anti-German cartoons*, with title: Gli unni . . . e gli altri. Germans pictured as barbarians. Thirty-four items in paperbound book published by Rava and Co. of Milan in 1916, with the stamp of the Haupt-Archiv der NSDAP.

3760. Extensive collection of German New Year and other greeting cards, 1860-1921, *Printing samples* assembled by a German printers' union as study material. Mounted on sheets 27" x 19" and each sheet dated. Approx. 2,200 cards.

3808. Album of reproductions of photographs, paintings, and prints illustrating great events and personalities in *German history* from the Middle Ages to modern times. Approx. 110 reproductions apparently issued in sets by the Bildstelle of the Reichsfuehrung SS.

3809. Album of photographs of the visit of *Hermann Goering* and entourage to Greece, under the cover title: Studienfahrt 1934, Griechenland. Approx. 200 photos in album.

3810. Interior and exterior views of Carinhall, *Hermann Goering's* large and pretentious home. Seventy photos in three portfolios, chiefly by Ernst H. Boerner of Berlin.

3847. Album of photographs of the *wedding festivities of Hermann Goering* and his wife Emmy, 1935. Approx. 75 photos in album.

3848. Albums of photographs, 1934-36, of *hunting trips by Hermann Goering* and friends, at Rominten, E. Prussia, and Stainwild near Berchtesgaden. Approx. 150 photos in three albums.

3861. Miscellaneous lot of German albums, 1934-44, from the library of *Hermann Goering*. Approx. 500 photos in nine albums and one portfolio.

3897. Funeral of *Paul Ludwig Troost*, Nazi architect and artist, 1935. Elaborate ceremonial burial including wreath from Adolf Hitler. Approx. 50 uncaptioned photos.

3899. Collection of German portrait photographs, 1920-45, of German artists, chiefly musicians. Approx. 500 items. A few stamped: Haupt-Archiv der NSDAP.

3904. Rooms of the Landesanstalt fuer Volkheitskunde at Halle-Saale with exhibits showing the excellence of early German folk art and crafts. Archaeological remains found in Germany. Photographic exhibits purporting to show the superiority of the Nordic peoples. Seventeen photographs in album dated 1934, originally belonging to Heinrich Himmler.

3907. Exterior and interior photographs of buildings and ships designed by *Paul Ludwig Troost* in 1925-35. Approx. 75 photos.

3930. Visit of Baldur von Schirach, Reichsjugendfuehrer, to a *Hitler Youth* camp in Stolberg im Harz, Germany, 1936. Seventeen photos presented to von Schirach in 1936.

3934. Collection of photographs of the ceremonies and activities of the *Hitler-Jugend* and of Reichs-

jugendfuehrer Baldur von Schirach, 1936-39 (?). Approx. 85 mounted photos.

3951. German news photographs of the *invasion of Poland* in September, 1939, released with highly biased captions. Fifty-two photos.

3966. Small lot of photographs of country grammar schools used by *German colonists in Latvia*, 1935-45 (?). Twelve photos.

4031. Small lot of photographs of Franz von Papen 1918-33. Eleven photos. Rehse collection.

4032. *Early Nazi party* photographs, 1920-30. Fifteen photos.

Note: The following items have been selected from the lot numbers not yet covered by the published checklist. The information is taken from the cards in the Prints and Photographs Division, in some cases supplemented by reference to the originals. As is the case with the foregoing list, the items given here are only a sample.

4320. Munich, 1939. Views of the "Buergerbraeu," destroyed by a bomb in the attempt on Hitler's life on November 9, 1939. Thirty-seven photos, mostly captioned, from the Rehse-Archiv. Correspondence concerning damaged furnishings from the "Buergerbraeu" which were transferred to the Rehse-Archiv is in the Supplemental Reference File.

4589. Pictorial history of the rise of the Nazi Party in Germany, 1920-33. Approximately 50 photos mounted for exhibition. Haupt-Archiv der NSDAP.

4594. Reproductions of designs for the burial monument of Frau Inga Ley, wife of Robert Ley, 1943. Diagram of "Leyhof," the family estate. Nine items.

4639. Pictorial propaganda material, chiefly clippings, from World War I. Approximately 200 items, mounted. From the Deutsche Arbeitsfront (DAF).

4641. Aerial photographs and related material concerning World War I. Areas in Finland, France, Italy. Approximately 50 photos collected by the Kriegsministerium, Flugabteilung.

4673. Scenes in Tibet, 1930-33. German documentary photographs made by the Ernst Schaefer expedition to Tibet. Twenty-five photos.

4890. Photographic portraits, 1890-1929, alleged to represent parents and other relatives of Hitler. These were confiscated by the SD as they supposedly indicate Hitler's real family background. A covering letter and memorandum, together with an inventory of the items, by Reichsfuehrer SS Himmler to Sekretaer des Fuehrers Bormann, 23 January 1944, is in the Supplemental Reference File.

4912. *Deutscher Bilderdienst fuer die Schule*, herausgegeben von der Abteilung Wirtschaft und Recht im NSLB (Nationalsozialistischer Lehrerbund), Bayerischer Lehrerverein, 1933. Views of Potsdam, Nazi demonstrations, etc. Vol. 1 only.

5227. Portfolio of photographs, probably of the Haus der SS Ahnenerbe, Berlin, 1935-40 (?). Eighteen photos.

5460. Nazi leaders, assembled on November 8, 1939. Eight photographs in a portfolio from the Constantin von Neurath Collection.

Section IX—Music Division

In the Music Division is a large number of captured German recordings and monitored broadcasts, both on disks and on tape. The following is a sample of the holdings, organized alphabetically by country of origin of the broadcast. It should therefore be noted that speeches by exiles and prisoners of war are not listed according to the nationality of the speaker. Wherever no specific label is mentioned, the recording was made by "Sonderdienst Seehaus." The records are located on Tier 49 in the stacks of the Library of Congress. They are arranged by dates or by subject matter. Some of the records were placed in folders or in cardboard boxes which are numbered.

AUSTRIA

A. Individual Speeches

Speeches by pre-1938 Austrian Leaders:

Dollfuss, Dr. Engelbert, Austrian Chancellor (1933–1934).

Innitzer, Dr. Theodor, Cardinal.

Schuschnigg, Dr. Kurt von, Austrian Chancellor (1934–1938).

Starhemberg, Ernst Ruediger von, Leader of the Austrian "Home Guard" and Austrian Vice-Chancellor.

The above recordings bear the following labels: "Allgemeiner Deutscher Katholikentag," Vaterlaendische Schallplatten des Oesterreichischen Heimatschutz, "Vaterlaendische Front," and A. Burkl, Wien III., Gerlgasse 22 (Ton-Schnitt). All the recordings are undated. Some bear the stamp "Hauptarchiv der NSDAP-Muenchen, Barerstr. 15." (Box A II.)

Speeches by Austrian Nazi Leaders:

Frauenfeld, Alfred Eduard, Gauleiter of Vienna (1930). Record in folder stamped "Nationalsozialistische Filmstelle Gau Wien, Hirschgasse 25." Undated. (Box XXIX.)

Kothen, Hans J.H.K. von, Gauleiter of Carinthia and East Tyrol. Undated and unlabeled (possibly 1932–33). (Box XXXI.)

BULGARIA

Kasasov, Dimo, Bulgarian Minister of Propaganda, Sofia, September 23, 1944; one record, incomplete.

Muraviev, Kosta, Bulgarian Minister President (Sept. 1—Sept. 9, 1944). Sofia, September 4, 1944; one record.

CZECHOSLOVAKIA

Gaspar, Tido, Head of the Office of Propaganda of Slovakian Government. Pressburg (Bratislava), October 1, 1943; six records, incomplete.

EGYPT

Canellopoulos, Panayotis, Greek Minister of Defense, Cairo, June 8, 1942; four records.

Nashaat Pascha, Hassan, Egyptian Ambassador to Great Britain, Cairo, January 7, 1943; five records, incomplete.

Papandreou, George, Greek Minister President, Cairo, June 28, 1944; two records.

Sofoulis, Emmanuel, Greek Minister of Social Welfare, Cairo, February 28, 1943; three records.

Venizelos, Sophocles, Greek Minister of Marine, Cairo, May 29, 1943; two records.

FINLAND

Hakkila, Vainoe, Leader of the Social Democratic Party of Finland. Speech delivered in the Finnish Parliament, Lahti, January 29, 1944; four records.

Helo, M., Finnish Minister of Finance, Lahti, January 21, 1945; two records.

Linkomies, Edward, Finnish Minister President, Lahti, July 2, 1944; five records.

Paasikivi, Juko, Finnish Minister President, Lahti, Dec. 8, 1944; four records.

———, Lahti, February 7, 1945; three records, incomplete.

Rangell, Johan W., Finnish Minister President, Lahti, May 17, 1942; three records, incomplete.

Ryti, Dr. Risto, President of Finland, Lahti, January 1, 1942; one record, incomplete.

———, Speech delivered in the Finnish Parliament, Lahti, January 29, 1944; four records.

Takki, Kristian, Finnish Minister of Commerce and Industry, Lahti, December 6, 1944; two records.

Tanner, Vainoe, Finnish Minister of Food and Supply, Lahti, October 28, 1941; three records.

GERMANY

A. Individual Speeches

Amery, John, British Nazi collaborator, Berlin, November 28, 1942; four records.

Axmann, Artur, Reichsjugendfuehrer, Berlin, January 3, 1943; four records.

Backe, Herbert, Reichsminister fuer Ernaehrung und Landwirtschaft, Berlin, October 3, 1943; six records, incomplete.

———, Berlin, October 1, 1944; three records, incomplete.

———, Berlin, November 19, 1944; five records, incomplete.

Benn, Gottfried, "Totenrede fuer Klabund (Alfred Henschke)." Label: Die Neue Truppe, undated. (Box A); one record.

Breitscheid, Rudolf, SPD member of German Parliament. Label: SPD-Berlin, Homocord, undated, (Box A); one record.

Bruening, Dr. Heinrich, German Chancellor (1930–1932). Election Speech 1932. Label: AEG, March 11, 1932, (Box AEG); one record.

Crispien, Kurt, SPD member of German Parliament. Label: Dralostron, undated, (Box A); one record.

Doenitz, Karl, Commander-in-Chief of the German Navy, Address to the German People on July 21, 1944; one record (On reverse: A. Hitler).

Feder, Gottfried, co-founder of the Nazi Party. Commentary to the Nazi Party Program. Label: Nationaler Schallplattendienst, G.m.b.M., Berlin, undated.

Goebbels, Dr. Joseph, Reichsminister fuer Volksaufklaerung und Propaganda, Berlin, January 30, 1933; one record.

——— Proclamation and Order of the Day to troops in southeastern Europe ("Der Kampf Beginnt"): April 6, 1941.

——— "Zur Lage," February 28, 1945. (On tape).

——— Speech to Foreign Laborers, March 12, 1945; one record.

Goering, Hermann, Address to the German People, July 21, 1944, two records.

Grzesinski, Albert, Prussian Minister of Interior (1926–1930), undated; on reverse: Stelling, Johannes. Label: SPD-Berlin (Box A I).

Hilgenfeldt, Erich, Hauptamtsleiter fuer Volkswohlfahrt, label: "Grammophon." Undated. (possibly 1938). (Box XXIX.)

Hindenburg, Paul von, Speeches 1931-32. Label: "Hindenburg" one record (Box XXXI).

Hitler, Adolf, Speech at Sportpalast, Berlin, February 10, 1933; six records in folder.

——— Speech at Opening Session of German Parliament, Potsdam, March 21, 1933; six records in folder.

———— Speech to German Parliament, Berlin, March 23, 1933; 11 records, incomplete.
———— Speech at Harvesting Festival, Bueckeberg, October 4, 1936; four records in folder.
———— Speech at Funeral of Hungarian Prime Minister Julius Goemboes, Munich, October 6, 1936; one record in folder.
Hitler, Adolf, and Mussolini, Benito, Munich, September 25, 1937; four records in folder.
Hitler, Adolf, Speech to German Parliament, Berlin, January 30, 1939; complete series of records.
———— Speech at Danzig (Liberation), September 19, 1939; seven records in folder.
———— October 10, 1939; four records in folder.
———— Speech at Buergerbraeu-Keller, Munich, November 8, 1939; nine records.
Hitler, Adolf, "Proclamation of the Fuehrer," Berlin, June 22, 1941; four records, incomplete.
———— Speech in Sportpalast 'to officers" Berlin, February 17, 1942; series of pressings in sealed steel cases.
———— Address to the German People, July 21, 1944; one record (on reverse: Admiral K. Doenitz).
Leipart, Theodor, Chairman of the Freie Deutsche Gewerkschaftsbund (pre-1933); one record.
Loebe, Paul, President of the German Reichstag (1928-1933). Label: SPD-Berlin (Box A I).
Mussolini, Benito, "Arrival in Berlin," Berlin, September 27, 1937; two records in folder.
———— Speeches and Toast on occasion of Italy's withdrawal from the League of Nations, Venice, May 7, 1938; two records.
———— Berlin, September 18, 1943; six records.
Ribbentrop, Joachim von, Danzig, October 24, 1939; five records in folder.
———— "Memorandum" Berlin, June 22, 1941; eight records.
Schemm, Hans, Bavarian Minister of Education and Chairman of the NSLB. Speech at a Meeting of the Nationalsozialistischer Lehrerbund (NSLB), Leipzig, April 8-9, 1933; 22 records, (Box III).
———— Speech at a Meeting of the Nationalsozialistischer Lehrerbund (NSLB), Frankfurt, July 3-4, 1934; 12 records, (Box VI).
Schirach, Baldur von, Reichsjugendfuehrer, Speech at Solstice Festival of Hitler Youth and SS on the Zugspitze. Label: Deutscher Reichsrundfunk; June 21, 1938; six records in blue album, incomplete.
Seldte, Franz, Founder and Chief of the "Stahlhelm," undated, (pre-1933). Label: Bundesamt des Stahlhelm, (Box A); one record.
Sender, Toni, Social Democratic member of the German Parliament. Undated, (pre-1933). Label: SPD-Berlin/Homocord.
Severing, Carl, Reich and Prussian Minister of Interior. Undated (pre-1933). Label: SPD-Berlin/Homocord.
Streicher, Julius, Gauleiter of Franconia, undated (possibly 1936); 13 records, incomplete, (Box XXIII).
———— Undated, (possibly 1936); 16 records, incomplete (Box XXII).
Toller, Ernst, author, pre-1933. Label: Die Neue Truppe; one record (Box A I).
———— "Drei Stuecke aus dem Schwalbenbuch;" one record, (Box A).
Taubert, Eberhard, Ministerialdirektor in the Ostabteilung of the Reichsministerium fuer Volksaufklaerung und Propaganda, Lecture on Soviet announcement of the dissolution of the Comintern. Label: Tonstudio Herbert Jacob, Berlin, May 26, 1943; two records.
———— , Interview, undated; one record.

Speeches by Austrian Nazi Leaders Recorded in Germany:

The following records bear the label: "An der schoenen blauen Donau, Walzer" (Blue Danube, Waltzes).

In reality, they contain speeches by Austrian Nazi who fled to Bavaria in 1935 where they engaged in illegal propaganda activities.
The speakers are:
Borek, Gauleiter of Upper Austria;
Habicht, Theo, Landesinspektor of Austria;
Hofer, Franz, Gauleiter of Tyrol and Vorarlberg;
Kothen, Hans von, Gauleiter of Carinthia and East Tyrol;
Pfeil, Deputy Gauleiter of Lower Austria;
Proksch, Alfred, Landesleiter of the Austrian Nazi Party;
Reuter, Walter, Stabsleiter of the Styrian Heimatschutz.

B. Special Events

Press Conference with Nazi Journalists in the Wuerttemberg-Baden Ministry of Propaganda. Label: Schallplattendienst of the Wuerttemberg Ministry of Propaganda. Undated (possibly 1933-34); three records (Box I).
Reichstag Session of March 21, 1933; five records, incomplete.
German News Broadcast. Official version of the Buergerbraeu plot, arrest of Georg Elser, etc., November 22, 1939; two records in folder.
German News Broadcast. Safe return of the German ship "Bremen," December 13, 1939; two records in folder.
Decorating Ceremony Broadcast. Two soldiers (Lt. Buss and Sgt. Slesina) of Propaganda Company 612 are honored, May 28, 1940; six records (Box XXXI).
Preliminary Franco-German Armistice Negotiations at Compiègne, June 21, 1940; 51 records (44 sides, in metal box).
Franco-German Armistice Negotiations and Signing Ceremony, Compiègne, June 22, 1940; 19 records (22 sides, in metal box).
"Christmas at the Front" Solstice celebration of soldiers in the field. Undated (possibly Dec. 21, 1940); four records (Box XXXI).
German News Broadcast on the Settlement of Bessarabian farmers on Polish Farms, Litzmannstadt, February 1941; 22 records.
German News Broadcast. War News, April 13, 1941; one record.
"Staatsakt" - Ceremony in the Foreign Ministry, Berlin, November 25, 1941; five records.
Speakers: Antonescu, Ion, Minister President and Foreign Minister of Rumania;
Lorkovitch, Mladen, Croatian Minister of Foreign Affairs;
Popoff, Ivan Vladimir, Bulgarian Minister of Foreign Affairs;
Ribbentrop, Joachim von, German Minister of Foreign Affairs;
Scavenius, Erik, Danish Minister of Foreign Affairs;
Tuka, Dr. Vojtech, Minister President and Foreign Minister of Slovakia;
Witting, Rolf Johan, Finnish Minister of Foreign Affairs;
"Berlin-Tokyo" Austausch-Sendung (Exchange Program), Berlin, January 20, 1942; one record, incomplete.
"Ten Years of History" radio propaganda broadcast tracing the rise of Germany from 1933. Undated (possibly 1943); 21 records (in metal box stamped: "Hauptarchiv der NSDAP).
Speakers: Hitler, Goebbels, and Goering.

Musical Recordings

"Jugend singt ueber die Grenzen (Youth sings over the frontiers). Group singing directed at Brazil and Yugoslavia. Label: Deutscher Rundfunk; one record in blue album.

Army, Nazi Party, Hitler Youth, Storm Troop, etc. songs and martial music. Labels: Gloria, Grammophon, Tempo, Nationale Tonplatte, N. S. Schallplattenindustrie, Telefunken, Patria, Homocord, Kristall, NSDAP - Record, Die Hakenkreuzplatte, His Master's Voice, and Schallaufnahmen des Deutschen Rundfunks; ca. 150 records (Boxes: VII, VIII, IX, X, XI, XII, XIII, XIV, XVI, XXV).

Folk music (German and non-German). Labels: Deutscher Rundfunk; Sueddeutscher Rundfunk; Westdeutscher Rundfunk; Lautarchiv; Institut fuer Lautforschung, Berlin; Nordischer Rundfunk, Hamburg; ca 60 records (Boxes XIX, XX, XXI).

GREAT BRITAIN

A. Individual Speeches

Arciszewski, Tomasz, Polish Minister President. London, December 7, 1944; two records, incomplete.

Benes, Eduard, President of the Czechoslovak Government, London, February 13, 1943; one record.
———, London, (via Moscow), December 21, 1943; three records.
———, London, January 28, 1944; one record, incomplete.
———, London, February 3, 1944; five records, incomplete.
———, London, February 4, 1944; two records.
———, London, February 5, 1944; two records, incomplete.
———, London, February 6, 1944; two records, incomplete.
———, London, February 8, 1944; two records.
———, London, June 10, 1944; one record, incomplete.
———, London, September 8, 1944; two records.

Galen, August Graf von, Bishop of Muenster, London November 22, 1941; three records.
———, London, January 11, 1942; two records.

Khan, Sir Mohammed Zafrullah, Agent-General for India in China, London, January 9, 1943; three records.

Masaryk, Jan, Minister of Foreign Affairs of Czechoslovakia, London, May 28, 1943; one record.

Michalopulos, Andre, Greek Under-Secretary of State for Information, London, May 21, 1942; two records.
———, London, April 7, 1943; two records.

Mikolajczyk, Stanislaw, Polish Minister President, London, May 3, 1944; six records.
———, London, September 1 1944; four records.

Nashat Pasha, Hassan, Egyptian Ambassador to Great Britain, London, February 11, 1943; six records.

Nemec, Frantisek, Minister of Economic Reconstruction of Czechoslovakia, October 4, 1943; two records.

Raczkiewics, Wladyslaw, President of the Polish Republic, London, September 1, 1943; two records, incomplete.

Sikorski, Wladyslaw, Polish Minister President and Commander-in-Chief, London, January 18, 1943; one record, incomplete.
———, London, February 10, 1943; two records, incomplete.

Simovic, Richard Dushan, Minister President of the Royal Yugoslav Government, London, September 3, 1941; two records.
———, London, February 19, 1944; two records incomplete.

Slavik, Dr. Jurai, Minister of Interior of Czechoslovakia, London, May 10, 1943; two records.

Subasic, Ivan, Minister President of the Royal Yugoslav Government, London, July 9, 1944; one record.

B. Special Events

Russian Special Message ("Russische Sonderbotschaft".) London, March 7, 1945; one record, incomplete.

HUNGARY

Baky, Ladislaus, Hungarian Minister of the Interior, Budapest, September 22, 1944; one record incomplete.

Kallay, Nicholaus, Hungarian Minister President and Minister of Foreign Affairs, Budapest, June 13, 1943; two records.
———, Budapest, September 1, 1944; two records, incomplete.

Kolozsvary-Borcsa, Mihaly Ritter von, Hungarian Minister of Interior, Budapest, September 3, 1943; two records.

ITALY

Badoglio, Pietro, Italian Minister President, Rome, August 18, 1943; one record.

Ciano di Cortellazzo, Galeazzo, Italian Foreign Minister, Rome, December 11, 1942; two records.

(Graziani, Rudolfo (Neghelli, Marchese di), Minister of Defense in Mussolini's "Republican Fascist" Administration, Rome, September 25, 1943; seven records incomplete.

Mussolini, Benito, Rome, December 11, 1937; one record in folder.

JAPAN

A. Individual Speeches

Bose, Subhas Chandra, Chief of the "Free India Provisional Government," Tokyo, June 22, 1943, Speech in English and German; seven records, incomplete.
———, (Speech in German). Tokyo, December 25, 1943; one record.
———, (Speech in Hindustani), Tokyo, December 25, 1943; one record.
———, (Speech in German), Tokyo, December 1, 1944; three records, incomplete.

Koiso, Kuniaki, Japanese Minister President, (Speech in German and Japanese), Tokyo March 11, 1945; six records.

Shigemitsu, Mamoru, Japanese Minister of Foreign Affairs, Tokyo, September 27, 1943; two records, incomplete.

Togo, Shigenori, Japanese Minister of Foreign Affairs Tokyo, January 19, 1942; four records.

Tojo, Hideki, Japanese Minister President, Tokyo, January 21, 1944; two records.

B. Special Events

"Berlin-Tokyo" (Exchange Program or Austausch-Sendung), Tokyo, June 29, 1942; two records.

Broadcast of Opening Session of Japanese Diet, Tokyo, January 28, 1943; two records.

"Berlin-Tokyo" (Exchange program, or Austausch-Sendung), Tokyo, March 15, 1943; 13 records, incomplete.

RUMANIA

Antonescu, Mihai, Deputy (and Acting) Minister President of Rumania, Bukarest, September 6, 1942; nine records, incomplete.
———, Bukarest, October 31, 1942; three records, incomplete.

SOVIET UNION

A. Individual Speeches

Ackermann, Anton, member of the Nationalkomitee Freies Deutschland, Moscow, October 23, 1943; two records, incomplete.

Hohmann, Heinrich, Major, member of the Nationalkomitee Freies Deutschland, February 19, 1944; two records.

Klein, Mattheus, member of the Nationalkomitee

Freies Deutschland, November 14, 1943; two records.

Korfes, Dr. Otto, Major General, member of the Nationalkomitee Freies Deutschland, Moscow, January 22, 1944; two records.

Lattmann, Martin, Major General, member of the Nationalkomitee Freies Deutschland, Moscow, March 25, 1944; three records.

Molotov, Viacheslav Mikhailovitch, People's Commissar of Foreign Affairs, Moscow, June 18, 1942; nine records, (on reverse: Zhdanov).

Potemkin, Vladimir P., Deputy Commissar for Foreign Affairs, Moscow, September 21, 1942; two records, incomplete.

Schroeder, Johannes, German Army Chaplain, member of the Nationalkomitee Freies Deutschland, November 23, 1942; two records, incomplete.

————, Moscow January 24, 1944; two records.

Seydlitz, Walter von, General, Vice-President of the Nationalkomitee Freies Deutschland, January 30, 1944; three records.

————, February 22, 1944; two records.

Shcherbakov, A. S., Secretary of the Moscow Committee of the Communist Party, Moscow, June 18, 1942; four records.

Stalin, Joseph, Chairman of the Council of People's Commissars, Moscow, November 6, 1941; four records, incomplete.

————, Moscow, November 6, 1942; eight records.

————, Moscow, November 6, 1943; eight records.

————, (Speech in German translation), Moscow, November 7, 1943; four records, incomplete.

Zhdanov, Andrei Alexandrovitch, member of the Politbureau, Moscow, June 18, 1942; nine records, (on reverse: Molotov).

B. Special Events

Soviet Propaganda Broadcast, Kuibyshev, February 7, 1942; six records, incomplete.

Ukrainian Program ("Ukrainische Sendung"), Moscow, August 30, 1942; 10 records.

Anti-Fascist Demonstration of Sportsmen ("Antifaschistische Kundgebung der Sportler"), Moscow, August 2, 1943; 22 records, incomplete.

Russian-Jewish Demonstration ("Russisch-juedische Kundgebung"), Moscow, April 2, 1944; 23 records, incomplete.

TURKEY

Inonu, Ismet, President of the Turkish Republic, Ankara, November 1, 1944; eight records.

Sarajoglu, Sukru, Turkish President of the Council, Ankara, February 21, 1943; two records.

Yucel, Hasan Ali, Turkish Minister of Education, Ankara, April 27, 1942; five records incomplete.

YUGOSLAVIA

Nedić, Milan, head of the German Puppet Government of Serbia, Belgrade, February 10, 1943; one record.

Section X—Newspaper Division

NOTE: Bibliographical information on microfilms of captured German scientific, technical, and economic material can be found in: *Bibliography of Scientific and Industrial Reports*, prepared by Office of Technical Services, U. S. Department of Commerce. This is the list of Publication Board (PB) reports from which the following are taken.

PB 46

"Concentration Camp Neuengamme, near Hamburg." Report dated 14 May, 1945: found complete records of the Neuengamme works of the Deutsche Erd- und Steinwerke G.m.b.H. — a subsidiary controlled by the SS Wirtschafts- und Verwaltungshauptamt (WVHA). Also found some personal letters of Oswald Pohl of the WVHA. Documents of the WVHA, Deutsche Ausruestungswerke had been removed, supposedly to the Organization Todt (OT), Einsatzgruppe, Niebuehl, Husum.

All principal documents found were turned over to Property Control, 609 MG Detachment in Hamburg.

PB 56

"Reichsvereinigung Eisen (RVE), S. W. District: Data on Condition of Documents." Report dated 11 April 1945:
1. Office of RVE and Haus Technik. Documents of value evacuated to Heidelberg.
2. Office of Dr. H. Roehling (Roechling ?). Documents of value also evacuated to Heidelberg.
3. Reichsgruppe Industrie. "A few routine documents were found."

PB 88

S. Brumer. "Oberstes Parteigericht in dem Kloster Schweikelberg." July 1945. In the Kloster Schweikelberg are records of Greifelt, Reichskommissar fuer die Festigung des Deutschen Volkstums, evacuated from Berlin in 1944. No documents of the Oberste Parteigericht are believed to be there.

PB 84

S. Brumer. "Reichsminister fuer die Besetzten Ostgebiete." 1945. At Schwarzenberg/Miesberg is the library of Dr. N. Nikuradse who did research for the Ostministerium, Zentrale fuer Ostforschung, Abt. Kontinentaleuropaeische Forschung, under the pseud. 'A. Sanders.' There are no documents in this collection.

PB 88

Frame, T. H., and Bricer, J. F. "Statement on Documents of German Foreign Office Protocol Section Archives, Hotel Hapsburger Hof, Bad Gastein," August 1945. Geheimrat Ruhe of the Protocol Section gave them a list of the papers moved there from Berlin. The list checked with the documents there. The list is now with the CIC (CIC 75/239,9 Aug. 1945). The documents were left there; they "could be removed in a three-quarter ton truck."

This is Combined Intelligence Objectives Subcommittee Evaluation Report No. 240.

PB 364

"Reich Ministry of Armaments and War Production," May 28 — June 14, 1945. Appendix B, pp. 4-19 is a translation of a letter, Speer to Hitler, 19 April 1944.

PB 442

"Private Papers etc., from Himmler's House in St. Quirin." A list prepared 5 August 1945. Includes the following items:

1. File of ms. correspondence between Himmler and his parents, April 1934; January 1936.
2. Guests in 1932.
3. Schiesskladde Reichsicherheitsdienst, 1938-39.
4. Miscellaneous, mostly accounts of festivities accompanying visits of high personages, 1943.
5. Newspaper clippings, kept by Himmler's parents, concerning the political life of their son, in three files, 1933-34; 1934-36.
6. Correspondence, 1918-26.
7. Marked "Schiesswesen"; contains also miscellaneous documents concerning the history of the Himmler family.
8. Travels from 1930-34.
9. Photograph album.
10. Correspondence dating back to the First World War.
11. Miscellaneous correspondence.

(These are the most important of 29 items in the full list.)
"Nazi Party and NSDAP" literature from house of Max Amann (Party Press Chief) at Tegernsee.
Various books and
Erfassung fuehrender Maenner der Systemzeit (ordered by Goering, marked Secret). These materials were deposited, in one box, with Captain Laeke, Document Center of 7th Army, Munich.

PB 522 (also PB 1784)

"Methods of Influencing International Scientific Meetings as laid down by German Scientific Organizations," 8 August 1945.
Contains full German text of two documents of the Deutsche Kongresszentrale found in a file on a conference of 29 July to 1 August 1937:

1. Kongresswesen und Hohe Politik (in Appendix 1, pp. 12-18).
2. Richtlinien fuer die Leiter deutscher Abordnungen zu Kongressen im Ausland (in Appendix 2, pp. 19-32).

These were in the confidential files of Professor E. Ruedin, Deutsche Forschungsanstalt fuer Psychiatrie, Kaiser Wilhelm-Institut,

Munich. A summary in English with excerpts translated is included.

PB 2419

"Reports on the German Economic Situation," 1943/44. A translated and edited copy of:
Der Beauftragte fuer den Vierjahresplan, Der Generalbevollmaechtigte fuer Ruestungsfragen, Das Planungsamt. "Bericht zur Deutschen Wirtschaftslage 1943/44," 29 June 1944 (Pla. 07222/29.6.); pp. 87.
A foreword explains the editing and nature of the document.

PB 2420

"Reports on the German Economic Situation." 1944. This is a report partly prepared during the war and partly worked on for the Allies after the war. It is a translated, edited, and completed copy of:
Der Beauftragte fuer den Vierjahresplan, Der Generalbevollmaechtigte fuer Ruestungsfragen, Das Planungsamt. "Bericht zur Deutschen Wirtschaft 1944;" pp. 26. A foreword lists those parts completed during and after the war. Cf. PB 2419.

PB 6656

"Examination of Dr. Ing. W. Osenberg. Dr. Osenberg was an official of the Planungsamt of the Reichsforschungsrat. This report records in detail the file system and document holding of Osenberg's office. 35 pages.
(NOTE: A large part of the documents of the Reichsforschungsrat appear to have been taken to the United States, incorporated in the form of individual items in the PB series, and deposited in the Library of Congress, Government Documents Section, to be serviced by the Newspaper Division. A few of these which are of general, non-technical, interest are cited here. For a complete listing it is necessary to check the various issues of the *Bibliography of Scientific and Industrial Reports* cited at the beginning of this section of the bibliography.)

PB 12745

"Administrative Correspondence, Haus der Forschung, Liaison and propaganda organization of the Reichsforschungsrat."
A folder of administrative correspondence, 1943-44 of the Reichsforschungsrat, Leiter des geschaeftsfuehrenden Beirats (Ministeraldirigent Mentzel).
(NOTE: This is the original folder.)

PB 12749

"Reichsforschungsrat administrative correspondence relating to utilization of the service of interned Dutch scientific workers." Original folder of the Praesident des Reichsforschungsrats, Leiter des geschaeftsfuehrenden Beirats (Mentzel), "Einsatz internierter Niederlaender." 1943-44.

PB 12755

"Discussion of security measures within the Reichsforschungsrat." Original folder of the Praesident des Reichsforschungsrats, Leiter des geschaeftsfuehrenden Beirats (Mentzel): "Abwehr." 1943-44. A folder concerning security measures in the Reichsforschungsrat, including some memoranda on excessive secrecy in research.

PB 12843

"Plans for the organization of an institute of scientific-technical news-reporting." Original folder of the Praesident des Reichsforschungsrats, Leiter des geschaeftsfuehrenden Beirats (Mentzel): "OKW." 1943-44. This folder contains a section entitled "Betr.: Prof. N. Bohr, Kopenhagen." This section includes documents on Bohr's leaving Denmark and his trip to England and the United States in 1944. His importance as a nuclear physicist is recognized.

PB 13177

"Reichsforschungsamt und Deutsche Forschungsgemeinschaft. Finanzierung einer wissenschaftlichen Arbeit des Ostinstituts," Juli 1937-Sept. 1938. A captured file concerning the financing of a study "Der sowjetische Raum als geowirtschaftliches Problem" by the Ostinstitut in Wannsee in 1937-38. The project was secret. There is no material on the study itself. Correspondence of the SS Hauptamt and other agencies concerning the financing of the project and the auditing of its books.

PB 13825

"Briefwechsel mit dem Reichsfuehrer SS." Original folder of SS Ahnenerbe, Reichsgeschaeftsfuehrer (Sievers): "G/SCH/4/r 3 Reichsfuehrer-SS." Correspondence between Ahnenerbe and other SS offices, mainly Reichsfuehrer-SS, Persoenlicher Stab, concerning combating of flies and mosquitoes, 1942-43.

PB 13178

"Oberkommando der Kriegsmarine, Deutsche Nordatlantische Expedition." Original folder of Praesident des Reichsforschungsrats, Leiter des geschaeftsfuehrenden Beirats (Mentzel): 1937-42. Miscellaneous correspondence with the German Navy.

PB 17638

"Geschaeftsordnung fuer den 2. Admiral der Unterseeboote." A photostat, 80 pp. Issued by von Friedeburg, 2. Admiral der Unterseeboote, 16 Sept. 1941.

PB 19221

"VDI (Verein Deutscher Ingenieure) Administrative Correspondence and Activity Reports." Original folder of Reichsforschungsrat, Leiter der Fachsparte Physik (Gerlach). Correspondence with the Verein Deutscher Ingenieure (a section of the Nationalsozialistischer Bund Deutscher Technik) 1944-45.

PB 27805

"Library, Deutsches Museum, Muenchen. Zugangsbuch-Serien." Accession record of the library of the Deutsche Museum, Bibliothek, on microfilm. 1832-1946.

PB 73518

"I.G. Farben A.G. Volkswirtschaftliche Abteilung. Berichte." Microfilm; the most important are (with frame numbers):

1-10 Liste der wichtigsten chemischen Unternehmungen Bulgariens. Feb. 1939.
72-93 Zypern. June 1939.
94-108 Der Aussenhandel Belgisch-Kongos. June 1940.
109-138 (31 frames) Die Kolonialmandate in Afrika. June 1940.
138-154 (30 frames) Ueberblick ueber die Wirtschaft Rumaeniens. March 1943.
174-184 (16 frames) Anglo-Aegyptischer Sudan (Wirtschaftsuebersicht). Oct. 1940.
185-196 (21 frames) Transnistrien, (Gebiet, Bevoelkerung, Wirtschaft). Oct. 1941.
197-205 Die chemische Industrie Ungarns. Aug. 1938.
206-229 Ziele des spanischen Wirtschaftsaufbaues. Oct. 1940.
591-626 Die deutsch-belgischen Handelsbeziehungen. Jul. 1939.

PB 73576

"I. G. Farben. Volkswirtschaftliche Abteilung." Economic reports on various countries. 1937-38.

1808-1930 Wirtschaftsbericht Norwegen.
1931-2058 Wirtschaftsbericht Neuseeland.
2059-2109 Das Erdoel des Orients.
2457-2570 Wirtschaftsbericht Palaestina.
2571-2526 Wirtschaftsbericht Polen.

PB 73841

"I. G. Farben. Economic reports."

3799-3921 Wirtschaftsbericht Ungarn. 1939.
4166-4251 Kato, H., Manschukuo (Fuehrer durch die mandschurische Wirtschaft). 1937.
4544-4629 Spaniens Wirtschaftskraefte. 1938.
4630-4687 Die Wirtschaft Nigerias. 1939.
4688-4735 Wirtschaftsstruktur der Tuerkei. 1937.

PB 73960

"I. G. Farben. Volkswirtschaftliche Abteilung." Text in German, English titles.

1819-1884 Economic capacity of Ireland.
2097-2108 Structure and importance of Italian industry.
2109-2152 The most important enterprises of the Rumanian chemical industry.
2215-2226 Economic structure and economic position of Venezuela.
2352-2360 Population of the Soviet Union according to the census of 1939.
2361-2438 Power, economy, and mining in Japan, Manchukuo, and Northern China.
2601-2711 Spanish economy after the Civil War.

PB 73961

"I.G. Farben. Wirtschaftliche Abteilung."
Text in German.

4371-4393 Methods of the English economic war. 1939.
4394-4438 The Economy of Portuguese East Africa (Mozambique). 1940.
4465-4491 Six additional frames. Locations of plants of the chemical and related industries of the USSR. 1942.
4506-4534 Economic statistics of Eastern Europe 1938.
4535-4539 The phosphates of the Soviet Union and their production. 1939.
4540-4563 Plants of the chemical and related industries in the USSR. 1942.
4563A-4565 The German raw materials supply from the USSR and eastern Europe. 1939.
4625-4628 Chromium ore production and foreign trade of the Soviet Union. 1940.
4628A-4663 Brief survey of the politics and economy of Greece. 1939.
4663A-4676 Energy and raw materials of the Soviet Ukraine. 1939.
4708A-4715 Economic structure and position of Sweden. 1938.

PB 73968

"I.G. Farben. Economic reports 1939."
Text in German.

722-755 Minerals in the Caucasus (excluding gasoline).
784-789 The economic structure and economy of Turkey.
790-794 Foreign trade of the US with USSR.
801-804 Manufacture and foreign trade of USSR with important raw materials, semi-manufactured goods and finished merchandise during 1935.
815-825 Foreign trade of USSR with chemical products.
826-831 Rubber industry in the USSR.
832-846 Views ot the development of the calcinated soda industry in the USSR.
847-866 Economic structure of Rumania considering territorial changes.

PB 74092

"I.G. Farben. Economic reports on various countries 1938-40." Text in German.

1-180 Economic reports on Argentina.
181-281 Economic reports on Afghanistan.
282-396 Economic reports on Egypt.
397-530 Economic reports on Belgium.
531-710 Economic reports on Brazil.
711-511 Economic reports on Bulgaria.
512-961 Economic reports on Colombia.

PB 74155

"I.G. Farben. Economic reports on various countries, 1937-46." Text in German.

2327-2891 Economic reports on Sweden.
2892-3061 Economic reports on Sudetenland annexed by Germany.
3062-3147 Economic reports on Thailand.
3148-3345 Economic reports on Switzerland.
3346-3468 Economic reports on Czechoslovakia.
3469-3798 Economic reports on Turkey.

Section XI—Manuscripts Division

The following is a list of the units which constitute the German holdings of the Manuscript Division. To a considerable extent these collections have not yet been finally organized; nor do they include all of the material eventually to be deposited there. The materials listed here are, nevertheless, now accessible in the Division. For ready location of individual documents, careful attention to the various numbers given for each group is absolutely essential.

1. *The Deutsches Auslande-Institut Collection.* This is a collection of large sections of the files of the Deutsches Auslands-Institut, Stuttgart. A detailed list has been prepared as Appendix 1. Further materials are being added to this collection. The Non-DAI materials are to be removed and integrated into other units where this is possible. In other cases separate units may have to be established. (52-162.)

2. *The German Submarine Materials.* This is a collection of German submarine log books together with some other items, particularly material on German-Japanese technical cooperation during World War II. See Appendix 2.

3. *The Himmler Files.* Reichsfuehrer SS, Persoenlicher Stab, Schriftgutverwaltung. Large parts of the Himmler files in photostat form have been organized according to the original file system of the Persoenliche Stab. A few other items have been placed with this collection. A listing of the individual Himmler files is included in Appendix 3, together with the other items.

4. *The Rehse Collection.* The Library of Congress has received large sections of the historical archives of the Nazi Party contained in the combined Rehse Archiv-Hauptarchiv der NSDAP. Materials already processed in the Manuscripts Division are listed in Appendix 4.

5. *The Adolf Hitler Collection.* A group of items of or concerning Adolf Hitler. A detailed list will be found in Appendix 5.

6. *The Eher Verlag Collection.* A few items from the files of the Eher Verlag, the

publishing house of the Nazi Party, are listed in Appendix 6.

7. *The Rust Collection.* The Manuscripts Division has a small collection of papers and correspondence of the German Minister of Education Rust. This is mostly personal correspondence. See Appendix 7.

8. *Miscellaneous Items from the Government of the Third Reich.* A number of individual items captured in Germany has been put together under this heading. See Appendix 8.

9. *Reichsstudentenfuehrung.* Under this title, the library has organized the papers of two officials of the Reichsstudentenfuehrung. See Appendix 9.

10. *Reichsarbeitsdienst.* Miscellaneous items from sections of the Reichsarbeitsdienst. See Appendix 10.

11. *Miscellaneous German Army Material.* A group of individual items of or connected with the German Army. See Appendix 11.

12. *Miscellaneous German Navy Material.* Various German Navy items other than those grouped in the Submarine Collection (No. 3). See Appendix 12.

13. *Miscellaneous German Air Force Material.* A collection of unrelated items. See Appendix 13.

14. *Einsatzstab Reichsleiter Rosenberg.* Items from the Einsatzstab and its Ostbuecherei. See Appendix 14.

15. *Very Old German and Polish Material.* See Appendix 15.

16. *Miscellaneous Old Manuscripts, partly unidentified.* See Appendix 16.

17. *Miscellaneous Technical Materials.* See Appendix 17.

18. *Wholly Miscellaneous.* See Appendix 18.

19. *The SS Ahnenerbe.* Carbon copies of administrative correspondence, 1941-43. Ten loose-leaf binders. Location: II, 38, 0, 1-2.

20. *The Munich Radio.* Letters confiscated in Munich from the Munich radio. Administrative files and correspondence, 1943-45. Fourty folders. F-1713.

21. *Ohnesorge Material.* Twenty-three binders of personal correspondence, 1916-43. Also a few other private items. To be added to this: Ohnesorge material including material on the Reichspostministerium in World War I. Various other personal items illustrating Ohnesorge's career as Reichspostminister. 52-162, 52-179. The photographs from this collection are listed under Prints and Photographs Division, Item 3480 (see above, Section VII).

22. *Dachau SS Court.* Three boxes of a card file of the SS Court at Prien.

23. *Goering Material.*
1. Jagd-Tagebuch (of purely personal interest). 9119.
2. Parchment award. 9342.
3. Personal notebook (of purely personal interest). 52-178.

24. *The Fritz Wiedemann Papers.* Five shelves of correspondence folders and boxed miscellaneous material. Mostly personal and business matters. The two folders labeled "Halifax" contain clippings. The "Hohenlohe" folder contains clippings and carbons of small personal items, for the most part. Some material on the suit of Princess Hohenlohe against Lord Rothermere. The most interesting material, much of it political, is in the box labeled "Private Papers." This box includes documents on Wiedemann's mission to London in July, 1938, and some memoir material. 9427.

25. *Gerdy Troost.* A very large collection of material from the Atelier Gerdy Troost. A great deal of material on the construction and designing of various Nazi buildings; personal and financial papers, correspondence, drawings, etc. 9491, 52-10.

26. *German Consulate Yokohama.* Two boxes of financial and marriage records of the German consulate in Yokohama. 9462.

27. *Allgemeiner Deutscher Gewerkschaftsbund.* Two correspondence folders of the Vorstand of the Allgemeiner Deutscher Gewerkschaftsbund (German Trade Union Federation), 1928-32. 52-179.

28. *NSDAP, Institut zur Erforschung der Judenfrage.* A considerable group of files and papers of the Institut. Dated ca. 1937-43. Not yet analyzed. 52-162 and 52-179.

29. *Akademie fuer Deutsches Recht.* A small group of typed protocols of sessions of various special subject committees of the Akademie. 52-162.

30. *Volksbund fuer das Deutschtum im Aus-*

land. A group of items additional to those now included in the Rahsa and DAI collections. 52-162.

31. *Anton Schaefer Papers.* A large collection of the papers of Anton Schaefer, official and member of parliament of the Deutsche Sozialdemokratische Arbeiterpartei in der Tschechoslowakischen Republik. These papers date back into the period of the Austrian Empire (ca. 1912), and run up to about 1936. Important for domestic political history of Czechoslovakia. 52-162.

32. *Sonderdienst Seehaus.* A large collection of official German monitoring reports in binders. Most of these are apparently the Sonderdienst Seehaus, first of the Auswaertige Amt and then of the Reichssicherheitshauptamt, Section VII. The material is organized chronologically, 1937-43. 52-179. (The regular, bound, mimeographed Sonderdienst Seehaus is accessioned in the Library of Congress as a serial and listed in the card catalog under Funkabhoerberichte.)

NOTE: The Manuscripts Division has a copy of the world list of the members of the Nazi Party outside of Germany. This list is based on the captured Nazi Party files in Berlin and was prepared by OMGUS, 7771 Document Center. The names are in alphabetical order and there is a country key. G 1668.

Appendix 1

DEUTSCHES AUSLANDS-INSTITUT (DAI), Stuttgart

CONTAINER NUMBER	DESCRIPTION	ACCESSION NUMBER
	MAIN OFFICE *General correspondence*	
1-2 Letter Binders	General correspondence, 1923-1940.	F-144, 8393
3-4 Letter Binders	Correspondence of the Secretariat of the DAI, 1940.	8393
4A (Box 848)	Correspondence of DAI officials with Lorenz, head of the Volksdeutsche Mittelstelle, one folder, 1937.	52-162
	List of members of the "Arrow-Cross" movement (Hungarian Fascist party), February 1942.	52-162
	DAI and the N.S. Frauenschaft, material concerning Lehrgaenge, one folder.	52-162
5-8 Letter Binders	Internal correspondence of the DAI, 1938-1942.	8393
9-11 Letter Binders	Correspondence concerning youth activities, 1938.	8393
12 Letter Binder	Correspondence concerning job applications, 1922-1929.	F-144
13 Letter Binder	Correspondence and other papers of a member of the Directorate of the DAI, 1930-1934.	8393
14 Letter Binder	Correspondence concerning manuscripts, 1915-1932.	F-144
15 Letter Binder	Correspondence of the DAI Office; Hauptabteilung Wanderungsforschung und Sippenkunde, 1938.	8393
16 Letter Binder	Correspondence concerning invitations, acceptances and reservations, 1937.	8393
17 Metal edge box	Correspondence concerning calendars. Correspondence concerning propaganda. Miscellaneous correspondence and manuscripts of the DAI.	8393
18-20 Letter Binders	Miscellaneous correspondence, 1935-1943.	8393
21-28 Letter Binders	Official correspondence files of Dr. Csaki, Director of the DAI, 1938-1943.	F-144, 8393
28A Letter Binder	Six more Csaki files, 1938-1943.	52-162
28B Letter Binder	Private correspondence of Dr. Csaki, including important political items. One file, 1936-37.	52-162
29-31 Metal edge boxes	Files of Dr. Bofinger, an official of the DAI and head of the Stuttgart Radio station. See also 52-179 at end of list.	F-144
32 Metal edge box	DAI files on various subjects.	F-144
33 Letter Binder	Note on the progress of the DAI filing system.	8393
	General Office Material	
34 Letter Binder	Copies of DAI bills.	8393
35 Metal edge box	DAI accounts, 1939-40. Bank accounts of the DAI. DAI bills. File on office supplies. File on pensions. Correspondence with Gestapo, and material concerning security regulations. Copies of documents, 1939-40, including a translation of Molotov's speech of August 31, 1939.	8393, F-144
		52-162
36 Letter Binder	Employment records of the DAI.	8393
37 Metal edge box	DAI office information concerning files and forms. Miscellaneous file of the DAI. Personal files containing list of DAI sections.	

	Officers of the DAI. Miscellaneous DAI materials.	8393, F-144
	File concerning Oskar Hartung, 1939–41.	52-162
Museum		
38–62 Letter Binders	General Correspondence of the museum, 1934–1939. Alphabetical arrangement.	8393
63–68 Letter Binders	Correspondence between the museum and the Volksbund fuer das Deutschtum im Ausland, 1934–42. Alphabetical arrangement.	8393
69 Letter Binder	Correspondence of an official of the museum.	8393
70 Letter Binder	International memoranda of the museum.	8393
71 Letter Binder	Material of the DAI Secretariat concerning the museum.	8393
72 Letter Binder	Museum correspondence concerning expositions and travel reports.	8393
73 Letter Binder	Museum correspondence concerning expositions and performances.	8393
74–75 Letter Binders	Correspondence with Nazi agencies, 1937–1938.	8393
76 Letter Binder	Correspondence of the museum with Nazi women's organizations.	8393
77 Letter Binder	Correspondence with other museums.	8393
78 Letter Binder	Correspondence of the museum with and concerning soldiers.	8393
79–80 Letter Binders	Correspondence between the museum and antique and book stores.	8393
81 Letter Binder	Orders for material by the museum.	8393
82 Letter Binder	Acquisition papers of the DAI Museum.	8393
83 Letter Binder	Correspondence of the museum concerning technical matters.	8393
84 Letter Binder	Miscellaneous museum correspondence.	8393
85 Letter Binder	Inventories of the museum.	8393
86 Letter Binder	Museum bills.	8393
87 Letter Binder	Museum file of duplicates of bills and accounts.	8393
Exhibitions		
88 Letter Binder	Correspondence concerning exhibits, 1939–1941.	8393
89 Letter Binder	File on various exhibits, 1921–1933.	8393
90 Letter Binder	Special exhibitions, 1938–1941.	8393
91–92 Letter Binders	Files on Slovakia, 1941–1943.	8393
93 Metal edge box	Material concerning Slovakia exhibit, Frankfurt exhibition of 1922.	8393
94 Letter Binder	Correspondence concerning Sudeten German exhibit, 1938.	8393
95 Letter Binder	File concerning exhibit about the farm buildings in Europe.	8393
96 Metal edge box	Holland exhibit, 1941. Exhibitions of Dutch art, 1942. Exhibition material, 1935–1937. Material concerning exhibitions, 1940–43. Miscellaneous museum material. Material concerning exhibits.	8393
Publications		
97–99 Letter Binders	Letter files concerning the DAI magazine, 1939–1942.	F-144
100 Metal edge box	Correspondence concerning publications, 1928–1931. Material covering publications of the DAI. Publication services of the DAI. Correspondence concerning missing books. Literary contest material. Material concerning prize contests. Material concerning literary prizes, ca. 1940.	8393, F-144 52-162
101 Letter Binder	Correspondence with publishers concerning an annual literary prize, 1940–1942.	8393
102–03 Letter Binders	Correspondence concerning publishers.	8393
104 Letter Binder	Correspondence concerning periodicals.	8393
105 Letter Binder	Correspondence concerning printers, 1941, 1942.	8393
106 Letter Binder	International publications of the DAI.	F-144 8393
Music Section		
107 Letter Binder	Correspondence of the central secretariat of the Music Section, 1940–41.	8393
108 Letter Binder	Correspondence of the Music Section with the Nazi Party, 1939–1941.	8393
109 Letter Binder	Correspondence with publishers concerning music.	8393
110 Letter Binder	Correspondence concerning choirs.	8393
111 Letter Binder	Collections of folk and country songs, 1935–1940.	8393
(Box 348)	Music of Germans outside Germany, 1938–1940.	52-162
112 Letter Binder	Contest of German composers outside Germany.	8393
113 Letter Binder	Unidentified file concerning music.	8393
Radio Section		
114 Letter Binder	Correspondence of the Radio Section, 1935–1939.	F-144
Miscellaneous		
115 Letter Binder	Miscellaneous manu-	

(Box 348)	scripts and reports of the DAI. Register of maps received, 1943-1943.	8393 52-162

LOCAL OFFICES OF THE DAI

Correspondence and other papers
DAI correspondence with:

116 Letter Binder	Augsburg to Berlin, 1940-1942.	8393
117 Letter Binder	Bremen to Darmstadt, 1939-1942.	8393
118 Letter Binder	Dornbirn to Hamburg, 1940-1942.	8393
119 Letter Binder	Insterburg to Karlsruhe, 1940-1942.	8393
120 Letter Binder	Kassel to Krakau, 1940-1942.	8393
121 Letter Binder	Muenchen to Neuberg, 1940-1942.	8393
122 Letter Binder	Reichenberg to Stein, 1940-1941.	8393
123 Letter Binder	Stettin to Weimar, 1939-1942.	8393

Files of the DAI offices at:

124 Metal edge box	Augsburg and Berlin, 1938-1941.	
125 Metal edge box	Berlin (regarding Germans in Russia) Bremen, 1938-1941.	8393
126 Metal edge box	Breslau, Danzig, Darmstadt, and Dornbirn, 1938-1941.	8393
127 Metal edge box	Dresden and Flensburg, 1938-1941.	8393
128 Metal edge box	Halle, Hamburg, and Hannover, 1938-1941.	8393

DAI Correspondence with:

129 Letter Binder	Hannover, 1939-1941.	8393

Files of the DAI offices at:

130 Metal edge box	Hohenzollern, Insterburg, Kaiserslautern, and Kassel, 1938-1941.	
131 Metal edge box	Leipzig, Magdeburg, Muehlhausen, Muenchen, Muenster, Passau, Posen and Reichenberg, 1938-1941.	8393
132 Metal edge box	Stettin, Stuttgart, Warnemuende, and relations with other offices, 1938-1941.	8393
133 Metal edge box	Weimar and Wien, 1938-1941.	8393

DAI Correspondence with:

134 Letter Binder	Wien 1939-1942.	8393

MATERIAL CONCERNING GERMANS ABROAD

By Countries

135 Scrapbooks	Two scrapbooks concerning German schools in Argentina.	8393
136 Letter Binder	Manuscript material chiefly on Austria.	8393
(Box 348)	Manuscript on church conditions of Germans in Eupen and Malmedy.	52-162
137 Metal edge box	Germans in the Rosario section of Argentina. Germans in Brazil.	

	Material concerning Czechoslovakia.	8393, F-144
	Letter from Brazilian German to the DAI, 1944	52-162
138-139 Metal edge boxes	Folders of letters from France concerning prisoners of war and others missing on French territory.	F-144
139A-C Metal edge box	Same.	52-162
140 Metal edge box	Finland, Great Britain, and Greece.	F-144, 8393
141-143 Metal edge boxes	A series of studies on Germanism in the Balkans, especially Hungary.	8393
144 Metal edge box	Germans in Hungary. Articles concerning Germans in Hungary. Photostats of a study of the names of the officials of the town of Fuenfkirchen (Pees), Hungary, 1933-42.	8393, F-144 52-162
145 Metal edge box	"Namenliste" of Germans in Mexico. Peru folder. Re-emigration of Germans in Russia. "Ost-Abteilung" (Germans in Russia). Photostats of old records of German colonies in Russia. Re-emigration of Germans from Russia, 1931-1933.	8393 52-162
146-154 Metal edge boxes	Reports from villages and cities settled by Germans in Russia. A series of Ortsberichte from individual villages, chiefly Ukrainian, prepared by Reichsministerium fuer die besetzten Ostgebiete, Sonderkommando zur Erfassung und Pflege des Deutschtums in den besetzten Ostgebieten, Kommando Dr. Stumpp.	
154A (Box 348)	Carbons of correspondence of Kommando Dr. Stumpp, 1943. Administrative records of Kommando Dr. Stumpp, 1943. File concerning a research and archive establishment in the Ukraine, prepared by Dr. Stumpp, 1942 (See also Box 335.)	8393
155-156 Metal edge boxes	Genealogies of Germans living in Russia; undated in alphabetical order.	52-162
157 Metal edge box	File cards on Germans living in Russia. German-Americans of importance to the work of the DAI. Folders on Germans in Russia, 1943. Material on Germans in Russia, 19th and 20th Century. Register of towns in Slo-	F-144 F-144

	vania, 1940. List of German settlements in southeastern and eastern Europe, and in Belgium.	52-162
158 Metal edge box	Slovakia Transylvania (economic) and the United States.	F-144, 8393
158A-C Metal edge box	Material concerning the United States.	52-162
159 Scrapbook	Transylvania (Religious material)	F-144

East and Southeast Europe

160-153 Metal edge boxes	Material sent to the DAI by the Volksdeutsche Mittelstelle concerning Germans in east and southeast Europe. Chiefly information forms (completed) concerning these people. No general arrangement. Re-Germanisation and repatriation files on Germans, probably in repatriation camps.	8393
160A (Box 348)	See above.	
184-243 Bundles	Same as above. This material is in general alphabetical arrangement.	8393
244-246	See above.	
247-248 Metal edge boxes	Questionnaires concerning Germans in the East (Europe). Material concerning Germans living in eastern Europe, 1939-1945. Correspondence, lists, etc., from the Russian Section of the DAI.	F-144, 8393
247A	Correspondence concerning re-settlement of Germans in the East, 1940.	52-162
248A	Register of files of the "Ost" section of the DAI.	52-162
248 Metal edge box	Germans in southeast Europe. Germanism in the East. Trips to southeast Europe. Publication "150 Jahre schwaebische Kolonisten in der Bucovina, 1787-1937,"	8393, F-144
	Germans in southeast Europe, ca. 1930.	52-162

MATERIAL CONCERNING LOCAL AREAS

249 Metal edge box	Germans in Schleswig-Holstein. Material concerning an academy in Silesia. Student aid societies in Stuttgart. Photostats of old records. Clipping concerning the founding of Neuglueck. Early records and materials on Steyer. Material concerning families in Unterschlecht-	

	bach. Listing of Jews in Stuttgart.	F-144

MATERIAL CONCERNING EMIGRATION

250 Metal edge box	Lists of Germans emigrating, 1907.	8393
251-253 Metal edge boxes	Passenger lists of Germans emigrating, 1908.	F-144
253A	Same.	52-162
254 Metal edge box	Collection of home addresses of Germans overseas by cities of origin, alphabetically arranged. Advice to Germans emigrating, 1923-1924. Miscellaneous material on Germans abroad. File on a few individual Germans overseas. Prominent Germans abroad, 1930's. Organisation of the biographical filing system. Office files of the "Sippenforschungsamt." Material for the biographical card file on individuals outside of Germany.	8393, F-144
	Questionnaire of Suabians outside Germany.	52-162
255-260 Metal edge boxes	Alphabetical card file of Germans overseas.	8393
261-263 Metal edge boxes	Card catalog, possibly of the DAI Library, arranged alphabetically by geographical areas.	

MATERIAL CONCERNING LOSS OF GERMAN CITIZENSHIP

264-265 Letter Binders	Loss of citizenship by Germans, 1937-1942.	F-144
266 Metal edge box	Letters about Germans who had lost their citizenship, 1937-1941. File of notifications of Germans who were no longer citizens of Germany, 1938-1942.	F-144

EDUCATION AND PROPAGANDA CONCERNING GERMANS ABROAD

267 Metal edge box	Education of various groups outside Germany: Individual national groups. Letters from Germans overseas applying to continue their education in Germany, 1932-1938. Propaganda material, 1940-1942.	F-144
268-269 Metal edge boxes	Education material	8393
269A	Courses in Germany for foreigners during vacations, 1937-1938.	52-162

MANUSCRIPT MATERIAL

270-271 Letter Binders	Material concerning prize contest for work on Germans overseas, 1942-1943.	8393
272 Metal edge box	Book reviews. Drafts of book reviews, arranged by issue, 1939. Manuscript of publication,	

"Ostpreussischer Heimatbrief Insterburg." Manuscript. "Der Sippenpfennig." Typed manuscript of book, "Dornbirner in aller Welt," by Dr. H. Lanzl.   F-144, 8393

272A A group of specialized manuscript studies about Germans outside Germany, ca. 1927. A paper on Yugoslav agrarian reform. Book reviews and plans, ca. 1935.   52-162

273 Metal edge box Miscellaneous manuscripts of the DAI. Page proof of an unpublished manuscript "Gottglaeubigkeit," manuscript of a book by Dr. Fritz Rumpf. Photostats of old manuscripts. Danzig and Mecklenburg   8393, F-144

273A Wilhelm Kurth, "Die Spaetgotische Kirchenbaukunst im Niederlaendischen Kuestengebiet." A Dutch manuscript.   52-162

273B Photostats of documents concerning Germans in or from Russia.   52-162

274 Metal edge box Photostat of miscellaneous manuscripts, chiefly 19th century. Miscellaneous manuscripts, drafts of articles. Miscellaneous manuscripts, no author given. Miscellaneous manuscripts   8393, F-144

274A Correspondence and materials concerning miscellaneous manuscripts, 1940. Miscellaneous manuscripts, two folders.   52-162

275 Metal edge box Miscellaneous manuscripts and papers. Unidentified manuscript, "Haendel - Zyklus." Manuscript. Manuscript material concerning German settlers of Engelsbrunn and Rosenberg.   8393, F-144

275A Part of a manuscript about the German archaeologist Heinrich Schliemann. Manuscript of Hans Hauerath, "Entwicklungsgeschichte des Germanischen und Deutschen Waldes, II. Die Geschichtliche Zeit." Manuscript of Hans Homberg, 1943, "Leistung durch Weisheit." Manuscript memoirs of Ludwig Edinger. Unidentified manuscript, 1942. Unidentified poems dating from the 1920's.   52-162

275 B Metal edge box Miscellaneous unidentified.   52-162

MISCELLANEOUS
Partially Identified

276 Metal edge box Unidentified work plan. Files of the Sippenkunde office DAI, drafts of forms. Miscellaneous correspondence. Unidentified personal file. Unidentified personal correspondence. History of the L. C. Hardtmuth firm. Material concerning the history of the Schleissing family. Material concerning the history of the Michalowsky family. Material concerning Mueller-Guttenbrunn. Chronicle of the Cossk family of Danzig. The Henrickson family, 1936. Register of lectures held, mainly on Germanism abroad, 1930-1940.   F-144, 8393   52-162

277 Metal edge box Miscellaneous records. Miscellaneous material. Miscellaneous concerning shipping.   8393

277A Miscellaneous material on German foreign policy, 1938-1940.   52-162

Press and Newspaper Material

278 Letter Binder Excerpts from Russian newspapers translated into German, December 1939-January 1941.   8393

278A Examinations of foreign newspapers, 1936-1939.   52-162

279 Metal edge box Reports on press and propaganda outside Germany. Clippings concerning the DAI. Clippings from the *Deutsche Zeitung*, 1937. Miscellaneous newspaper clippings, 1940-1942. Miscellaneous newspaper clippings and releases.   F-144, 8393

Religious Affairs

280 Metal edge box Bibliography on religious affairs. Copies of church records.   8393

281 Letter Binder File of listings of photostated church records.   8393

Photographs

282 Metal edge box Pictures of Germans prominent in the affairs of other countries. Biographical lists and descriptions of Germans prominent in the affairs of other countries. See above.   8393

283 Metal edge box Pictures of various countries in Europe. Picture file of German

	folk costumes from various parts of the world.	8393
284 Metal edge box	Miscellaneous photostats and pictures.	8393

Miscellaneous Card Files

285 Metal edge box	Bibliographical file on Germans overseas. Unidentified card file.	8393
286-289 Card Files	Card file of Germans overseas.	8393
290-295 Card Files	Miscellaneous unidentified card files.	8393
295A-C	Same.	52-162

MATERIAL FROM GERMAN ORGANIZATIONS TURNED OVER TO, OR ACQUIRED BY, THE DAI; OR RECEIVED WITH DAI MATERIAL

Waffen SS Material

296-302 Metal edge boxes	Material concerning the indoctrination of foreign units of the SS, 1943-1945.	F-144
	Miscellaneous SS material, 1944.	52-162
303 Metal edge box	Miscellaneous SS material. Police file on Wildhagen case. SS material from southwest Germany. Captured Russian book listing disposition of Russian troops in White Russia and mobilization schedules in 1936. Miscellaneous SS material.	F-144
304-306 Metal edge boxes and 306A	SS monitoring reports of foreign radio broadcasts and newspapers; Sonderdienst Seehaus.	8393

Nazi Party Material

309 Metal edge box	Miscellaneous Nazi Party and SS documents. Includes some papers of Martin Bormann. Foreign units of the Waffen SS. Speech of Albert Speer. List of speeches of Nazi Party officers, 1940-1944.	8393, F-144
	File of the NSDAP, Kanzlei, III D, concerning training of soldiers, 1943-1944.	52-162
310 Letter Binder	File of Reichskanzlei concerning the Autobahn, ca. 1932-1943. Includes photostats of orders signed by Hitler.	
311-312 Metal edge boxes	Nazi Party Records; badly damaged by fire.	F-144
313 Letter Binder	Financial records, forms and directives of the Nazi Party (Reichsschatzmeister) 1937-1943.	8393

Army and Luftwaffe Material

314 Letter Binder	Secret folder regarding damage by air raids to industrial areas. From the High Command of the Armed Forces (OKW). Not identified.	

	Table of contents included. 1944.	8393
315	Intelligence report of damage at the Gerhard Fieseler Werke, 1943-1944.	8393, F-144
Metal edge box	Personnel and administrative records of German anti-aircraft unit, 1943-1945.	8393, F-144 52-162
	Miscellaneous papers of the High Command of the German Army, (OKH). Numbered list of documents. Administrative records of a German unit in Russia; Note: This organization compiled the reports from Russian cities and villages settled by Germans, Boxes 146-154, which see.	8393, F-144 52-162
315A	Administrative records, der Reichsminister der besetzten Ostgebiete. 1942.	
	Personnel and administrative records of German anti-aircraft unit, 1943-1945.	8393, F-144 52-162
316 Scrapbook	Scrapbook and Regimental History of the German Infantry Regiment 110, 1936-1938.	8393
317 Metal edge box	German Air Force intelligence report on Polish aircraft industry. List of damaged office equipment from Allied raid on Ludwigshafen, April 16-17, 1943.	8393
318 Letter Binder	Records of German aircraft production compiled by U. S. Strategic Bombing Survey.	8393

I. G. Farben Material

(No connection with the DAI, but received with it.)

319-325 Letter Binders	Records of I.G. Farben	8393
326 Metal edge box	Information about chemical processes and air-raid precautions. I. G. Farben material. I. G. Farben proposal to Russia on making synthetic gasoline from coal, Nov., 1939. I. G. Farben; pictures of plant. Correspondence and circulars concerning air-raid protection.	8393
	I. G. Farben, lecture on the European economy, 1943.	52-162

Miscellaneous

327 Letter Binder	Gestapo records of Darmstadt, 1943-1944.	8393
328 Letter Binder (in safe 5B, 2)	Secret file of the Ausland-Abwehr, Abt. Ausland III. Regulations concerning the strength of units and lists of the Abwehrstellen all	

	over Germany (by Wehrkreis) and in all of Europe; gives number and positions of men, number and kind of weapons, and number and kind of vehicles. 1942-1944.	8393
329 Metal edge box	Indexes of material turned over to the Rehse Collection. Military records from World War I. Folder of material on hunting. Awarding of medal, 1917. Miscellaneous unidentified folders.	8393, F-144
	Material of the Institut fuer Grenz- und Auslandsdeutschtum (Marburg).	52-162
329A	Material of the Volksbund fuer das Deutschtum im Ausland.	52-162
329B	Same.	52-162
329C	Accession records of a library. Chronicle of events in Bessarabia, May 1939 - November 1940, by Pastor Rivinius. Record of periodical subscriptions. Glossary of terms.	52-162
330 Letter Binder	Unidentified letter file.	8393
331-344 Volumes	Concerning Germans and German settlements abroad.	8393
345 Card File	List of DAI material identified by Mr. Lederer in 1946. See Section I.	8393
346-347 Wooden boxes	Contain unidentified catalogs.	8393
348 Metal edge box	Items which could not be placed into containers 4A, 111A, 115A, 136A, 154B, 160A, 183A.	52-162
349-359 Metal edge boxes	The Zimmermann Collection. This collection contains material concerning Transylvania in the 19th century.	8393, 52-162
359A Metal edge box	Nachlass Elia Triebnigg-Pinkhert. mostly material on Germanism in southeast Europe and Turkey, 1849-1949.	52-162
360-364 Metal edge boxes	Papers of Dr. Alfred Bofinger 1919-1940. Includes correspondence, notebooks, manuscripts and personal miscellany.	52-179

Appendix 2

The German Submarine Materials. Ac. D.R. F-1850, 2366

(NOTE: The following is a list prepared by the Manuscripts Division of the Library of Congress.)

Box	Contents	Date
1	Industrial information transmitted to the Japanese.	ca. 1944
2	Industrial information transmitted to the Japanese, seven folders.	ca. 1943-44
	Contract between the German Government and the Japanese Navy concerning exchanges of patents and raw materials.	1944
	An envelope of material for the German Naval Attaché in Tokyo.	1943-45
	A bundle of material for the Japanese.	1944
3	Industrial information transferred to the Japanese.	1944
	Folders containing correspondence concerning military deferments of the Reichsforschungsrat.	1942-43
4	Private files of Rear Admiral Loewisch, German Naval Attaché in Rome.	ca. 1939-42
5	Material concerning "U-234."	1941-45
6	Material concerning "U-505."	1941-45
	Material concerning "U-505." Radio Log Books.	1941-45
7	Material concerning "U-505." Radio Log Books.	1941-45
8	Material concerning "U-505." Radio Log Books. Battery Check Book. Commissary Account Book.	1941-45
9	Material concerning "U-505."	1941-45
	Material concerning "U-530."	1941-45
	Material concerning "U-505."	1941-45
10	Material concerning "U-505."	1941-45
11	Material concerning "U-505."	1941-45
12	Material concerning "U-505."	1941-45
	Material concerning "U-858."	
	Material concerning "U-873."	1941-45
	Material concerning "U-967."	
13	Material concerning "U-967."	1941-45
	Rough Logs	
	Material concerning "U-977."	
	Log Books	1943-45

NOTE: The continuation of this list will be found on p. 74.

Appendix 3

HIMMLER FILE

Container No.	Folder No.	Contents	Dates
1	1	Miscellaneous	1938-42
	2	Miscellaneous.	1942-43
	3	SS Standarte Nordland.	1940
	4	Miscellaneous.	1935-43
2	5	Sterilization.	1934-38
	6	Slovakia.	1940-45
	7, Mappe 1	Hungary.	1939-43
3	7, Mappe 2	Hungary.	1944-45
4	7, Mappe 2	Hungary.	1944-45
	8	Rumania.	1939-45 (mainly 1942-45)
	9	Church Matters.	1928-43
	10	Orphans in East Germany.	1942
5	11	Miscellaneous, includes material on the Flemish SS, Slovakia, propaganda leaflets, Russian, German, English, etc.; includes material from Folder 12.	1940-44
	13, Mappe 3	Netherlands.	1944-45
6	14	Alsace-Lorraine and Luxembourg.	1942-44
6	15	Hunting invitations, records, etc.	1934-42

Box	Folder	Mappe	Contents	Dates
	16		Winterhilfe collections, etc.	1937-42
7	17, Mappe 1		France.	1942-44
	17, Mappe 2		France.	1942-44
	18		Headquarters building for the SS.	1941-44
	19		Reich finances.	1942
8	20		Germanic volunteers.	1942-44
	21		General administrative matters.	1941-42
	22		Miscellaneous.	1939-45
	23		German unit from Nikolaev.	1942
	24		Individual letters of complaint to the SS.	1944-45
9	25, Mappe 1		Norway.	1941-44
	25, Mappe 2		Norway.	1944-45
	26		Soviet Union.	1941-44 (Some back to 1335)
	27		Miscellaneous industrial affairs.	1942
	28		Illegitimate children in the Occupied Eastern Territories (slip says file removed).	
	29		SS unit from Steyer.	1941-42
	30		Care of inventors (slip says file removed).	
10	31		Miscellaneous.	1942-43
	32		Miscellaneous.	1938-44
	33		Material concerning accidents.	1941-44
	34		1) Agricultural policy.	1938-42
			2) Population problems.	1938-42
10	35, Mappe 1		Correspondence with and reports of the Reichskommissar fuer die Festigung deutschen Volkstums (Greifelt).	1942-43
	35, Mappe 2		Same.	1944
11	36		Party and Army Courts.	1935-42
11	37		Organization of supply for the Waffen SS in the East.	1942
	38		Correspondence of Himmler with Goebbels concerning radio stations.	1941-42
	39		Agriculture and rationing.	1942-44
	40		Material concerning occupied France, particularly Lorraine.	1941-44
	41		Miscellaneous.	1942-43
	42		Miscellaneous.	1943-45
12	43		Correspondence with and about the Volksdeutsche Mittelstelle (Lorenz).	1942-45
	44		Collections of used clothing, shoes, paper, etc.	1943-45
	45		Correspondence with and about the circle of friends. (Freundeskreis) of Himmler (Kranefuss).	1942-44
	46		Material on health matters.	1942
	47		Correspondence with and concerning the SS publication "Schwarze	

Box	Folder	Contents	Dates
		Korps" (d'Alquen).	1938-43
	48	Correspondence with and concerning Hauptamt fuer Volkswohlfahrt der NSDAP (Hilgenfeldt).	1937-43
	49	Pictures and one letter concerning colonial policy.	1942
13	50	Dental care of the SS.	1940
	51	Miscellaneous.	1941-?4
13	56	Danmark.	1941-43
	57	Material concerning Occupied Eastern Territories; relations Reichsfuehrer SS - Ostministerium.	1942-44
	58	Reports on internal conditions and morale in England.	1941-44
	59	Construction matters.	1941-44
14	60	Reichsparteitag.	1941
	61	Miscellaneous.	1941-44
	62	Miscellaneous.	1941-44
	63	Material on the world ice situation (Welteislehre).	1938
	64	Spain.	1940-44
	65	Decoded Spanish telegrams.	
	66	Correspondence with or about the Ahnenerbe	1942-43
15	67	Concentration camp matters.	1938-44
	68	Reports and other material on the situation in occupied France and Belgium.	1941-44
	69	German and foreign propaganda; morale at the front.	1942-44
16	70	Miscellaneous, some correspondence with German Foreign Office.	1942-43
	91	Miscellaneous.	
	92	Empty.	
	93	Administrative correspondence with Greifelt, two items.	1942
	94	Folder re. re-settlement and extermination of Jews	1941
	95	Administrative matters re. SS economic administration in occupied territories.	1942-45
17	96	Order concerning packages on courier plane.	1942
	97	German group from Palestine, to be settled in the Crimea.	1941-43
	98	Foreign radio reports concerning Himmler.	1942-44
	99	Promotions.	1942-44
	100	Re-settlement of Tyrol Germans.	1941-44
	101	Miscellaneous administrative matters.	1942-44
18	103	German agrarian matters.	1935
	104	SS administrative matters.	1941
	105	Reichskriegerbund (Kyffhaeuserbund).	1935-42
	106	Norwegian SS units.	1941-44

		boat.	1943
	214, Mappe 1	Care of German children in Norway.	1942-43
	214, Mappe 2	Case of SS officer Tondock.	1943-45
	215	Problem of land ownership in the Occupied Eastern Territories.	1942-43
	216	Administrative letter.	1942
	217	File on the bomb attack on Hitler, 20 July 1944. Taken out by the Politische Adjutantur.	
26	218	The winter battle of Rshev.	1942
	219	Italy.	1942-44
	220	Miscellaneous.	1943-44
	221	Establishment of camp for Rumaenische Legionaere (Iron Guard).	1942
	222	Investigation into an army camp.	1943
26	223	Various requests and suggestions of Himmler.	1943
	224	An article about ship construction.	1942
27	240	Miscellaneous.	1938-45
	241	Awarding of Golden Party Emblem.	1943
	242	Investigation of anonymous complaints.	1943-44
	243	Missing.	
	244, Mappe 1	Labor and slave labor.	1942-44
	244, Mappe 2	Labor and slave labor.	1944
	245	Missing.	
	246	Bugattiwerk (Trippolwerke) in Molsheim in Alsace.	1940-44
	247	Personnel and administrative matters.	1942-45
	248	The SS Cavalry Division.	1943
28	249	The Kriegsversehrte.	1943-44
	250	Miscellaneous.	1942-45
29	—	Duplicates of folders 32-36.	
G-622		Transcript in German of Heinrich Himmler's notebook containing remarks about books he read in the years 1926-34. The original notebook (written in shorthand, "Gabelsberger" system) is said to be in the hands of the U. S. Army in Berlin.	

To be added to the Himmler Collection:

51	179	Folder of SS directives of the SS Leibstandarte "Adolf Hitler".	1938-34
52	162	SS administrative records.	1944-45
52	162	A register of the orders and decrees of the Reichsfuehrer SS for the years	1939-40
52	162	An envelope containing material concerning anti-resistance terror in Belgium with handwritten notations of Himmler's decisions on these matters.	1944
52	179	Folder of material concerning book loans of the library on the Soviet Union of the Reichssicherheitshauptamt, Amt VI.	1943-44 (*)

Appendix 4

Rehse Collection
Accession D.R. 52-10

Container Number	Contents
1	Munich Police File: Ernst Toller.
2	Munich Police File: 1. Felix Fechenbach; 2. Gustav Landauer; 3. Dr. Karl Liebknecht; 4. Rosa Luxemburg.
3	Munich Police File: 1. Kurt Eisner; 2. Erich Muehsam.
4	1. One folder re. E. Kroemmelbein. 2. Two folders re. Professor Stempfle. 3. One folder re. Erich Muehsam.
5	1. Dietrich Eckart material re. Raete-Republik (Communist Government) in Bavaria, dat. 1923. 2. Two folders of manuscripts, correspondence, photographs, etc. re. Dietrich Eckart.
6	1. Archiv: F. J. Rehse, "Zehn Jahre Deutsche Geschichte." 1914-1924. 2. Membership and identification cards and contributions of Rehse. 3. Folder: Buergerrat Muenchen and the Nazi Party, 1922-1923.
7	1. Instruction book on military training in Augsburg, Sept. 1838. 2. Material pertaining to the Franco-Prussian War, 1870-71. 3. Copy of a letter to the Prussian (?) King, 1875. 4. Ms. plan for German action in India, 1914. 5. Four folders of miscellaneous material, some pertaining to World War I, discussing rationing, how to protect oneself in an air raid, etc.
8	World War I material. 1. Orders of the First and Tenth Army Corps (German). 2. Junius Alter, "Das Deutsche Reich auf dem Wege der geschichtlichen Episode," 1916. (An attack on the policies of Bethmann Hollweg by Franz Sontag.) 3. Letters of Graf von Zeppelin, 1916, concerning annexations in the West, required for German security; also matters concerning air warfare. 4. Folder on unrestricted submarine warfare, World War I, 1916. 5. Strictly confidential account signed "E.R.", of a conversation with Adm. von Holtzendorff pertaining to U-Boat warfare. 6. Manuscript material concerning political matters during World War I (including U-Boat warfare). 7. Two folders of correspondence and manuscript material, 1914-1918. 8. Washington Alliance, 1916, an American organisation for keeping the U. S. neutral.
9	Miscellaneous material (mostly World War I).
9A	A combined diary and scrapbook of World War I.
10	Miscellaneous postcards of two war periods, 1914-1918 and 1939-1945.
11	1. Ms. of a play, "Die Werthern" by Leo Benario.

2. Postcards re. the attack on the Social Democratic party in Vienna, 1927.
3. Manuscript re. the attack of the Marxist press against the Nazi party.
4. Booklet on the Marxist press in Munich.
5. Roehm Putsch, June 30, 1934 (included is a partial list of the victims).
6. Miscellaneous material including papers pertaining to the putsch of November 9, 1923.
7. Booklet re. the November 9, 1923 putsch.
8. File of letters from people who could not attend a Nazi public exhibition.
9. Material concerning the Thule-Gesellschaft, 1920's.
10. Twenty Nazi songs in typescript and dedicated to Hitler.
11. Poem or song book.
12. Miscellaneous directives and plays.
13. Manuscript of book, *Geschichte der Loebener Burschenschaft "Germania"* by Rudolf Brier, 1924 (Ac. No. 9027).

12   Miscellaneous Nazi material, 1922-1940.(?)
13   Material re. Freemasonry.
14   Poems and letters sent to Hitler and Goebbels by their admirers (See also 22 I, 5 K.)
15   Birthday greetings, poems, letters, and compositions sent to Hitler and Goebbels by their admirers.
16   1. Press excerpts of the Rehse Collection, 1940-1941.
    2. Guide to newspaper clippings.
17   1. Translation of book reviews of *Mein Kampf.*
    2. Book reviews and notices of *Mein Kampf.*
18   Manuscript of Sven Hedin's book, *Deutschland und der Weltfriede.*
19   Miscellaneous material.
20   Miscellaneous material.
21   Abgeordnetenhaus (unidentified), 1892.
22   1. Manuscript entitled, "Oeffentliches und
G 1530 privates Recht in der politischen Grundordnung" by Dr. Heinz Kummer, 1942.
    2. "Deutsche Katholiken und nationalsozialistischer Staat" by Joseph Kral, 1934. From the Library of the NSDAP. Reichsleitung, Buecherei, Stab des Stellvertr. des Fuehrers.
    3. "Der Christus des Nordens" by Paul Friedrich Lettow.
22A Eight volumes of photostats of letters of and
F 2899 concerning Dietrich Eckart, dated about 1913-1915.

Alt-Rehse Collection

23   1. "Ahnen-Pass" Books.
    2. Material pertaining to racial and ancestral lineage, by Prof. Boehm.

Miscellaneous Collection

(Much of this is Rehse material)
24   1. Register of secret patents, 1941-1942.
    2. General Gouvernment Institut fuer Deutsche Ostarbeit (Cracow). Inventory of Library.
    3. Volume of propaganda material.
25   Material sent to the Minister of Propaganda.
26   Nazi material.
27   Nazi material.
28   Files of the Nazi Party (arranged alphabetically).
29   Membership books (in various German and Austrian organizations).
30-31 Manuscripts and photostats of the Scharnhorst Papers from the Heeresarchiv, Potsdam. The United States National Archives has a collection of the Scharnhorst papers. The two boxes of Scharnhorst material in this collection, (52-10) may be either duplications or additions to the Scharnhorst material at the National Archives.

32   1. Photostatic copy of the Serbian reply to the Austrian ultimatum, July 1914.
    2. Miscellaneous material of World War I — including account books.
33   Miscellaneous material:
    1. A study of the First, Second, and Third Internationals.
    2. Chinese play in three acts.
    3. Folder on "wine culture."
    4. Japanese Seamen's Union material.
    5. Financial account of Japanese holdings (?).
    6. Folder pertaining to accident insurance, 1941-1942.
    7. Folder of unidentified miscellaneous material.
34   1. NSDAP, Reichsrechtsamt. Concerning Zentralarchiv fuer Politik und Wirtschaft.
    2. Volksbund fuer das Deutschtum im Ausland, Austrian Section, register of the Library.
    3. Extraordinary decrees of the President, 1930-1933.
    4. Verein zur Erhaltung des Deutschtums im Ausland, Landesverband Bayern, register of the library.
    5. Reform-Verein Deutsch-Oesterreich, library register.
    6. Contents of a staff Library in Munich, 1940.
    7. Von Stockhammern'sche Kriegsbibliothek, Index, 1940.
    8. Die Deutsche Arbeitsfront, papers from the library.
    9. A book: *Schwarzrote Kirschen* by Alexander Hunyadi, comes from the "Bibliothek zur Erforschung der Judenfrage" (Frankfurt a.M.)
35   1. Papers of Der Reichssparkommissar, 1931.
    2. Manuscript of a booklet entitled, "Supplying Germany with Gasoline."
    3. A manuscript of the book, *Einfuehrung in die Runenlehre* by Albrecht Diedrich Dieckhoff.
36-39 Letters received by, and papers pertaining to, Marburg University (mainly 1912-14).
40   Material concerning World War I.
41   Accounts of the Institut fuer Grenz-und Auslanddeutschtum.

ADDITIONS TO REHSE COLLECTION
Ac. D.R. 52-179

22B		
Correspondence of the Bund der Deutschen.	1933-37	
Newsletter of Jungvoelkischer Bund, Bundesamt.	1933	
Polish propaganda material from Danzig.	late 1930's	
Material on the Austrian Nazi Party.	1934-37	
German mimeographed announcements from occupied Poland.	1941-42	
Material of a Ukrainian youth organization in Cracow	1940's	
American Quaker Relief forms, World War I		
List of evacuated people to be billeted in Striega	1943-45	
Correspondence and other ma-		

terial of the Sudatendeutsche Heimatfront. — 1934-35

Material on the plebiscite in the Saar. — 1934-35

Voting papers for the Anschluss plebiscite of April 10, 1938. Material concerning the plebiscite in Upper Silesia. — 1922

22C-D Material of the Czech National Socialist Party. Organization folders of the party. Statistics of the party in various localities. — 1937

22E Material concerning the persecution of Czechs during World War I. Folders of the Czech National Socialist Party. Folder of Benes material. Folder of Thomas G. Masaryk material, chiefly congratulations. — 1922, '26 '35

Memorandum on future treatment of Slavic minorities in Hungary, addressed to the Hungarian Prime Minister. — 1922-36

Correspondence and files of the Czech League of Riflemen. — 1933

22F Folder of material concerning Czechoslovakia and Czech material turned over to the Rehse Collection. — 1937

Some files of the Nazi party in Czechoslovakia. — 1940

Regulations concerning establishment of the Nazi Party in Czechoslovakia — Deutsche Nationalsozialistische Arbeiterpartei. — 1930

Miscellaneous material of the Czech Communist Party.

A list of prices in Czechoslovakia. — 1941

Material of Josef Grohmann. Czech Nazi Party membership cards. — 1930-31

22G Files of the Sudeten German Party. — 1933-38

22H Nazi Poems and Songs. Collection of Nazi Songs. Ode to Hitler, in Italian, translated into German. Poem dedicated to Hitler. — 1939

Material from World War I. Miscellaneous from World War I. — 1916

Austrian military proclamation. — 1916

Austrian travel book. — 1847-65

Safe conducts from the occupied Rhineland. — 1919

Austrian passports. — 1914-20

Miscellaneous. Personal membership material in Austrian national organisations. Miscellaneous and unidentified.

22I Personal birthday congratulations to Hitler. (52-178). — 1932

22J Personal birthday congratulations to Hitler (52-178), includes a few to Goebbels. — 1932 & '30

22K Book of birthday congratulations to Hitler. — 1933

Birthday congratulations to Hitler. — 1932-37

Appendix 5

The Adolf Hitler Collection

Safe 5 1. A volume of the records of the Franz Eher Verlag listing sales of *Mein Kampf*, 1925-1933; also books by other Nazi leaders

Safe 5 2. Documents concerning the Hitler family, 31 pieces, mostly about Hitler's parents

Safe 5 3. American copyright application for *Mein Kampf*.

Safe 5 4. Nazi Party membership booklet of Julius Schreck, Hitler's driver.

Safe 5 5. Folder of Der Sekretaer des Fuehrers (a title created for Martin Bormann, NSDAP, Partei-Kanzlei, in 1943) on Hitler's daily activities, 30. Jan. 1934 to 30. June 1943; pp. 101. Title: "Daten aus alten Notizbuechern."

Safe 5 6. Box of miscellaneous Hitler items. There are several sketches, probably by Hitler, and some written notes for a speech, probably in Hitler's handwriting. There are several unidentified ms. items. The main identified item is a group of typed records of utterances of Hitler in January, 1942. They may be identified as follows:

1. Wolfsschanze, Jan. 8-9, 1942; pp. 9. *Note:* P. 1 is on the back of stationery of Der Leiter der Partei-Kanzlei (Martin Bormann).

2. Fuehrerhauptquartier, Wolfsschanze, nachts, Jan. 16-17, 1942; pp 16.

3. Wolfsschanze, nachts, Jan. 17-18, 1942; pp. 3. (concerns the set-backs in the winter war with Russia).

4. Fuehrerhauptquartier, Jan. 18, 1942; abends; pp. 4. (concerns German domestic politics — Papen, Hindenburg; Rumania; Hungary; England).

5. Wolfsschanze, Jan. 18-19, 1942, nachts; pp. 2.

6. Wolfsschanze, Jan. 19, 1942, abends; pp. 3 (concerns duels).

7. Wolfsschanze, Jan. 20, 1942, mittags, pp. 2 (Gast: RFSS Himmler); pp. 2. (concerns age and rank in the military service).

8. Wolfsschanze, Jan. 22, 1942, mittags (Gaeste: RFSS Himmler, Gauleiter Rainer); pp. 2., (concerns rule by Germans over others).

9. Fuehrerhauptquartier, Jan. 24, 1942, abends; pp. 2.

Safe 5 7. Negative prints of 8 handwritten postal cards from Hitler to Max Amann, 1917. (52-178)

Safe 5 8. Typed copies of the utterances of Hitler, 1942, under item 6 above. (52-178)

Safe 5 9. Photostats of manuscripts of Hitler, drawings, letters to, and manuscripts of other leading members of the Nazi Party. Includes photostats of originals in the Manuscripts Division. Misc. dates and undated. (52-178)

(52-178)
Box 1 — Bills to Hitler. — ca 1930-32
Box 2 — Telegrams and letters (with plans for answers) on the re-introduction of conscription sent to the Presidential Chancellery, 1935 Telegrams on the re-introduction of conscription sent to the Nazi Party Chancellery. — 1935
Manuscript, translation into Hungarian of Hitler's speeches. — ca 1940 & '43
Early photographs and clippings of Hitler. — 1901-32
Book of telegrams on Hitler's birthday. First

item is a telegram from Goering to Hitler, 1933.

To be added to the Hitler collection (now in Rare Books Division):

A group of photostats of German military records from World War I concerning Hitler's military service.

Appendix 6

Eher Verlag Collection
(Accession D. R. 52-10)

Container Number	Contents
48	Historical and statistical development of the Nazi Party Press, 1926–35. (Includes a manuscript and supporting data.)
49	Manuscript material of the Eher Verlag Collection.
50	1. Manuscript material of the Eher Verlag. 2. Manuscript material re Eugen Ritter von Schobert.
51–52	Auflagen-Uebersicht (Deutsche Zeitungen) 1937–38.
53	Register of a musical collection.

Appendix 7

Rust Collection
(Accession D. R. 52-10)

Container Number	Contents
42–44	Personal letters of Fraeulein Rust and family.
45	1. Education material. 2. Report card of Hildburg Rust.
46	1. Rust correspondence, 1942–44. 2. Postcards.
47	Photographs of the Rust family and acquaintances.

Appendix 8

Miscellaneous Items from Government of the Third Reich

Number	Description
8494	Guest Book of von Neurath. Dates from June 12, 1939 to September 24, 1941.
8770 Sale 5B-1	This item is a diary of Dr. Otto Braeutigam, Representative of the Ministry of the Occupied Eastern Territories (RMfdbO) to the High Command of the Army (OKH) June 11, 1941 to February 8, 1943. 1 vol.
G 243	Files of the Reichsministerium fuer Ruestung und Kriegsproduktion, Ruestungskommando Ulm (Donau), 1942–44.
8373	Documents from the Finanzamt Duesseldorf-Sued, 1944.
8373	Trip record, 1938–39, of a car belonging to the NSDAP, Gauleitung Franken.
8513	Photostats from the Reichskanzlei, 1942, concerning the award of the Kriegsverdienstkreuz 2. Klasse.
8513	Photostats of congratulations to Hitler on his birthday. No date is given.
8513	Cancellation of a lost pass to the Reichskanzlei, April 24, 1945.
E 1360	Two mss. (typewritten) in one volume sent to Hitler on his 50th birthday. 1. Author: Hanns Kerrl, "Weltanschauung und Religion." 2. Author: Hanns Kerrl a memorandum entitled "Die praktische politische Loesung der religioesen Frage im Dritten Reich," Nov. 1939. This volume is from the Partei-Kanzlei, Sonderbuecherei.
8070	Facsimile of a form letter NSDAP, Reichskriegsopferfuehrer, 1941.
52-179	Financial record book of the Reichskanzlei, 1889–1923.

Appendix 9

Reichsstudentenfuehrung

Number	Box No.	Description
8751	1-2	Loose-leaf manuscript notebooks. No. 1: correspondence file of Dr. Fritz Kubach, head of the Amt fuer Wissenschaft und Fachersiehung of the Reichsstudentenfuehrung, 1937-1939. No. 2: speeches by Dr. Fritz Kubach, 1934-1943.
8770	7	Correspondence of Dr. Erich Otto, 1934-1940, Reichsfachgruppenleiter Volksgesundheit. Files of Dr. Otto, 1933-1936.
8770	7	Files of Dr. Otto, 1935, concerning inheritance and racial matters, and files concerning financial matters, 1937-1939.
8578	3	Papers of Fritz Kubach. Diary, account book and notebooks. Lecture or report, probably by Kubach, from Otto's file, concerning functions of Section Volksgesundheit, Reichsstudentenfuehrung. Lecture on Education by Fritz Kubach. Lectures and correspondence of Kubach, 1942-1943. Papers of Kubach, 1941-1943. Correspondence of Kubach, 1943-44. Miscellaneous papers of Kubach, 1943. Material concerning Copernicus collected by Kubach.
8578	4	Kubach Family Papers. Chiefly correspondence, 1937-1943.
8578	5-6	Card files of Kubach (possibly of Otto).
8578	8	Papers of Erich Otto. Diary, account book, and medical book of Otto. File of Otto concerning the reorganization of medical education along Nazi lines, 1937. Medical material — two folders. Material of Erich Otto concerning the subject of haemophilia, 1938-1939. File of Otto's reports, 1934-1936. Correspondence of Otto, 1935-1939.
8578	9	Papers of Erich Otto. Papers of Erich Otto, 1934, '38, and '38. Correspondence of Erich Otto, 1935-37. Correspondence of Erich Otto, 1937. Correspondence of Erich Otto, 1937-38. Correspondence of Erich Otto, 1937-38. Correspondence of Erich Otto, 1934, '38 and 1940. Correspondence of Erich Otto, 1936-38.
8578	10	Miscellaneous. Item of German Propaganda Ministry, concerning forbidden literature, 1944. Two copies of a report on events in Austria went to the office of the Nazi Party for Austria in Munich (Landesleitung Oesterreich). Misc. volumes & notebooks.

Appendix 10

Reichsarbeitsdienst

Number	Description
8737	War diary 1 of: Reichsarbeitsdienst, Arbeits-October 12, 1942, in France and at Luftgau dienstgruppe K 341; November 16, 1940 to VII. Also minor papers.
8725	Contains one portfolio of materials of the Reichsarbeitsdienst (RAD). These are papers of the German Labor Service, 1941, 1944-45; they pertain to: relations between the Labor Service and Air Force; character and qualification ratings of officials of the Labor Service; miscellaneous affairs of the Labor Service; the teaching of history as a means of education.
8770	Membership book in the Reichsarbeitsdienst (RAD).

Appendix 11

Miscellaneous German Army Material

Number	Description
8737	Payments record of a German military unit in Salzburg, (1941).
8737	History of a battalion of the 716th German Infantry Division. From April 18, 1941 to April 23, 1943. Mostly stationed along the coast of France. (Index and text.)
8633	File High Command of the Army (OKH), ms of a book by Dr. Hoehne, "Der Feldverpflegungsbeamte," 3rd ed. 1941.
8779	Two items (military diaries). Five items (military identification books). One item (military driver's license).
8770	Ms. from Heereslehrer-Akademie (HLA), "Abteilung A, Ausbildung fuer den gehobenen Dienst."
9027	(a) Catalog system of Wehrkreisbuecherei V and (b) Index to part of catalog of Wehrkreisbuecherei V. (One container).

Appendix 12

Miscellaneous German Navy Material

Number	Description
9098	German Navy, Marinewerft Wilhelmshafen — concerning the construction of five oil tanks.
9098	German Navy, Marineneubauamt Nordholz—Plans for Wirtschaftsgebaeude. 1940.
9098	German Navy, log and repair books of German minesweepers M-589 and M-504.
8631	Correspondence file of the OKM, Marineoberkommando Sued, Druckschriftenverwaltung, 1944-45. Mostly about German naval units in the Adriatic Sea.
8737	Organizational chart of the Neptunwerft, 1938 and other items, 1937.
8737	Files of the Neptunwerft. Miscellaneous subject matter, (1938-39).

Appendix 13

Miscellaneous German Air Force Collection

Number	Description
9737	Folder of blueprints and plans of Dornier and Messerschmitt aircraft. Other miscellaneous materials in folders.
9098	German notebooks concerning organization and employment of the Radio Reconnaissance (Funkaufklaerungsdienst) of the Luftwaffe.
9098	Manuscript in French concerning maritime expansion of modern nations. The manuscript is from the Library of the Wissenschaftliche Gesellschaft fuer Luftfahrt, Berlin.
9098	Records of aircraft contracts with various concerns, 1937-38-39.
9098	German aircraft — technical material.
9098	Records of a German Anti-Aircraft unit, 1941.
8737	Letter from Reichsminister der Luftfahrt und Oberbefehlshaber der Luftwaffe, to: High Command of the Armed Forces (OKW), Wehrwirtschafts-und Ruestungsamt May 18, 1940, concerning imports of aviation gasoline from Russia and Rumania.

Appendix 14

Einsatzstab Reichsleiter Rosenberg
(52-179)

A. 1. File on Soviet Agriculture and Religion, 1943-44.
2. Copies of official decrees governing the activities of the Einsatzstab Reichsleiter Rosenberg.
3. Draft of publicity material on the organization, 1942.
4. Catalog system for books on the Soviet Union.

B. Files of the Einsatzstab Rosenberg, Ostbuecherei.
1. Register of literature on the Soviet Union, Parts 1, 2, 4.
2. Catalog of the Non-Russian Section of the Ostbuecherei.
3. Correspondence and other material, chiefly about book loans of the Ostbuecherei. Two folders. 1943-44.

Appendix 15

Very Old German and Polish Material

Number	Description
9137 Item 1	Regulations governing the performance of religious services in the chapel of the Moyland Patronage; late 16th or 17th century.
Item 2	Record of a private debt, late 15th century.
E 2790	Charter and seal granted to Masonic Order in Prussia by Frederick the Great, July 16, 1774.
8524 Item 1-6	Records of the local office in Grebenstein, Hesse-Cassel; dated 1772, 1764, 1763, 1717, 1692, 1709.
Item 7	Petition in Hesse-Cassel by a citizen for relief of payments imposed during the Thirty Years War, 1630.
C 1082	Documents from the archives of the City of Magdeburg, 15th and 16th century. (See attached list, sent by the unknown donor.)

8737 Partially typed and partially manuscript material, 1772-1778. In Latin and Polish. Change of sovereignty and transfer of allegiance from the King of Poland to Maria Theresa, Empress of Austria, in the First Partition of Poland for the province of Galicia. Copies from a document of the city of Lwow (Lemberg).

Contents of the Documents   (G 1082)

1. Document from November 26th, 1405. King Wenzel grants permission to Archbishop Guenther of Magdeburg to levy toll on every cart going to market.
2. Document from December 11th, 1449. Pope Nicolaus V. informs Archbishop Frederic of Magdeburg that a papal ambassador will arrive to discuss confidentially all matters pertaining to the church.
3. Document from September 17th, 1455. Pope Calixtus III informs the Archbishop of Magdeburg that a special ambassador will arrive with a confidential announcement.
4. Document from October 20th, 1455. The Synod of Basel informs Archbishop Frederic of Magdeburg that two clergymen will soon arrive from Basel to report on synodic discussions.
5. Document from December 12th, 1453. Bishop Burchardt of Magdeburg gives a fief to his follower Hennig of Neyndorf.
6. Document from September 29th, 1474. Duke William of Brunswick gives a fief to his cupbearer Hans of Neyndorf.
7. Document from September 28th, 1478. The cousins Hans and Hennig of Neyndorf transfer a part of their fiefs to Juergen of Bardelebbe with the approval of their lord, the Bishop of Halberstadt.
8. Document from March 12th, 1509. With the approval of the Archbishop of Magdeburg, Hennig of Neyndorf sells a part of his fiefs to the Deacon of Halberstadt.
9. Document from July 20th, 1531. Archbishop Albrecht of Magdeburg decrees a new tax for his subjects.
10. Document from May 19th, 1549. Emperor Charles V. confirms the granting of a salt tax to Archbishop Albrecht of Magdeburg which had been previously confirmed to his bishop predecessor.

Appendix 16

Miscellaneous Old Manuscripts, Partly Unidentified

Number	Description
8770	Unidentified manuscript (1826).
8770	Records of the Merstedt Family, 19th Century.
8541	Manuscript copybook (mathematics: algebra & geometry). First entry date is 1777.
8633	Unidentified 19th Century manuscript.

Appendix 17

Miscellaneous Technical Material

Number	Description
8033	German technical notes and drawings ca. 1941.
9098	Technische Hochschule in Darmstadt, 1937; papers of Walter Hess concerning cyclones; telephone register.
9098	Professor Schmidt, lecture on the "Theorie mechanischer Schwingungen," 1929-1930.
8737	Drawings seized at Heilbronn, technical.

Appendix 18

Wholly Miscellaneous

Number	Description
8714	Fuer CILLI und unsere Kinder. 1777-1932 (a typewritten manuscript; two copies). Personal memoirs of Dr. Hugo Heinmann.
9098	Manuscript notebook dealing with (names, addresses, and accounts) Indian Independence League.
9098	German logbook of incoming calls, 1943-44.
8737	Typed ms. by Maximilian Reidel, 1937-1942.
8129	Axis surrender documents (photostats).
8770	1 box: 5 folders. 1. Songbook of Isa Kroch. 2. (2 items) Ahnenpass of A. G. Bruegmann.
32-162	Miscellaneous papers: 1 container. Miscellaneous papers of World War I. Miscellaneous records of Brown, Boveri & Co. 1941-42. Material (possibly) of the Nazi Party in Austria, 1934. Material dealing with a German military school, 1937-38. Miscellaneous records, 1937.
8737	Folder of material from the Berlin office of the Tokyo Shimbun (in Japanese language), 1942-43.

Section XII—Exchange and Gift Division

Of the four Wehrkreis libraries which came to the Library - IV, VII, XII, XIII - two and parts of a third are still in crates in the care of this section.

Also there is a very large number of crates of material from the Rehse collection, contents unknown. One group of 20 crates has been opened. For contents see Appendix 1. The manuscript material in this has been transferred to the Manuscript Division.

There is a very large collection of press clippings, mostly still in crates. The bulk of this material probably comes from the Archiv der NSDAP. There are also smaller collections of newspaper clippings from such places as the Adolf Hitler-Schulen.

There are apparently also some other materials in the custody of this section, including parts of several German libraries, pre-World War I military records, and the library of Alfred Rosenberg.

All of this material is unregistered and unlisted. It is kept in the stacks of the annex.

Appendix 1

The 20 crates which have been opened

contain material from the Rehse collection - the historical archives of the Nazi Party. Parts of this collection have been previously distributed to at least the following divisions of the Library of Congress:

Prints and Photographs
Manuscripts
Music
Rare Books

I. POSTERS AND LEAFLETS

I. The overwhelming bulk of the material in the crates opened consists of posters and leaflets. Some, perhaps a quarter to a third of the total, are in well-defined and labeled units. From a third to half of the posters were found in groups of a fairly well-related nature. The rest were found disorganized (or had never been organized). The main period covered is from the beginning of World War I into the later years of World War II. The majority of the items are in German, but there are large numbers in Russian, Czech, French, Polish, and English, a few in Spanish, Dutch, and Hungarian, and a considerable number with parallel texts in German and one other language. The following groups of material, each of which consists of a sizeable amount, are representative:

1. Posters and leaflets illustrating the rise of the Nazi Party from its beginnings to 1933.
2. Posters and leaflets concerning the history of World War I, e. g. mobilization, war loans (German, American, French, Russian), military occupation, recruitment (all major powers).
3. Revolution in Germany — the various disturbances in Germany from 1918 to 1923, including the activities of the Soldiers and Workers Councils, the Spartacists (Communists), the various revolutions and counter-revolutions (e. g. Communist government in Bavaria, Kapp reactionary uprising in Berlin), the elections for the Weimar Constituent Assembly, etc.
4. Materials on the Allied occupation of the Rhineland after World War I and the French occupation of the Ruhr.
5. Posters, leaflets, etc. of all German political parties and associations — Communist, Socialist, Clerical, Nationalist, etc. of the Weimar period.
6. Materials on the Nazi regime, 1933-1943. Party rallies, plebiscites, "elections," collections for the winter help, and other Nazi functions.
7. Posters and leaflets illustrating the history of Austria-Hungary in World War I.
8. Posters and leaflets of the various political parties in Austria, 1918-38.
9. Posters and leaflets, as well as other materials, of the German parties in Czechoslavakia, particularly the Sudeten German Party of Henlein and the Communist Party, as well as of various Czech parties.
10. A group of Spanish Falangist materials from the Spanish Civil War.
11. Posters and leaflets from World War II, including:
    a. Announcements and decrees in territories occupied by the Germans (a large group, partly printed, partly mimeographed, often bilingual).
    b. German propaganda and recruitment posters put up in the occupied territories, a number of them in Russian.
       NOTE: For a comprehensive listing of the propaganda material of which samples are included in this group, see Germany, Reichsministerium fuer Volksaufklaerung und Propaganda, Abteilung Ost, *Lager-Verzeichnis Ostpropaganda*, "Nur fuer den Dienstgebrauch," (Berlin, 1943-44). (D810.P7G884.)
    c. Posters captured by the Germans, particularly in Russia.
12. A considerable number of commercial posters, particularly advertisements for cigarettes, fashions, and travel.

II. MAPS

A considerable number of maps, a large proportion in German. There is a group of operational maps from World War I. Of special interest is a group of captured Russian and Polish maps illustrating the campaigns of the Civil War, 1918-22.

III. CHARTS

There is a large number of charts of various kinds. They include architectural drawings and instructional charts. An example of the first would be some plans for the reconstruction of Berlin according to suggestions made by Hitler. A wall chart of the Nuremberg racial laws will illustrate the second.

IV. AIR PHOTOS

A few composite maps made out of photographs taken by reconnaisance planes and balloons in World War I have been grouped together.

V. RUSSIAN BULLETIN BOARDS

There is a group of Soviet bulletin boards,

containing pictures, slogans, bulletins, etc. which were presumably taken by the Germans from captured Soviet factories.

VI. MANUSCRIPTS (now in the Manuscript Division)

The manuscript material can be grouped into two parts. There is almost a crateful of files of the official German monitoring agency (Sonderdienst Seehaus) consisting of files of monitored broadcasts and newspapers.

There is a group of miscellaneous items including files of material of and concerning the Czech presidents Masaryk and Benes.

VII. NEWSPAPERS

There is a considerable pile of complete newspapers, mostly German.

VIII. NEWSPAPER CLIPPINGS

Many of the clippings are unfortunately loose, though mounted. A good proportion is either in folders or in binders on specific subjects.

IX. PRINTS AND PHOTOGRAPHS

Some loose and unorganized. A large number in unified lots, such as a group of pictures on American occupation forces in the Rhineland after World War I.

X. MIXED

A considerable number of folders contain materials of various kinds on one subject.

These include some of the most important materials in this collection. There are folders on various Communist parties and a very important collection of materials on the Kapp uprising of 1920. These folders may be kept as a unit and deposited with one division of the library.

XI. MUSIC

There are a couple of musical items.

XII. MISCELLANEOUS PROGRAMS

A large amount of miscellaneous material, consisting mainly of two groups of material:
a. Programs of performances in the Government General (German-occupied Poland);
b. Programs, special newspapers, etc. from and about carnivals (this is the bulk of this group).

XIII. PAINTINGS

A group of paintings seized by the Germans in Russia.

XIV. COINS

There are six German coins (turned over to the Smithsonian Institution).

XV. LAWS AND DECREES

There is a small group of serials of legal decrees, etc.

XVI. BOOKS AND PERIODICALS

All the books, pamphlets, and periodicals have been grouped together.

Chapter 4

NATIONAL ARCHIVES OF THE
UNITED STATES

THE captured German documents in the National Archives will be found in the following Record Groups:

1. Record Group 242: World War II Collection of Seized Enemy Records. The German material in this Record Group consists of two main sections. First, there are pieces of the Heeresarchiv Potsdam. For these the War Records Section of the National Archives has both some listings of its own and the original German deposit records. In Appendix 1 this material is listed by the name of the German under which the material is grouped with the amount of material for each name indicated. In the second place, there is a group of miscellaneous materials. These are listed in some detail in Appendix 1, as no comprehensive listing has been prepared by the National Archives for this section.

2. Record Group 243. Records of the United States Strategic Bombing Survey. See Appendix 2.

3. Records of the German Foreign Ministry. The microfilm copy of German Foreign Ministry records, received from the Department of State, can be briefly described as consisting of 176 rolls of 35 mm. positive microfilm, dating from June 1914 to October 1918. Continuous files in the Archives of the German Foreign Ministry are covered by several "serials" (film jobs). Each serial (except those in the 5276-5296 group, see Appendix 4), is spread over several containers. The microfilms transferred to the National Archives can be identified as follows:

1 "World War";	279 vols.; see Appendix 8.
2. "World War," Geheime Akten	39 vols.; see Appendix 4.
3. Peace moves of the Central Powers	18 vols.; see Appendix 5.
4. Mediation; peace moves and tendencies	87 vols.; see Appendix 6.
5. Mediation; peace moves and tendencies, "geheim"	54 vols.; see Appendix 7.
6. Outbreak of war	One vol.; see Appendix 8.
7. United States,	Two vols.; see

Aug. 1917 - Oct. 1918   Appendix 9.

NOTE: Record Group 260, Records of the Office of Military Government for Germany, does not contain captured German documents.

Appendix 1

Potsdam Heeresarchiv, Record Group 242, in charge of the War Records Section.

Boyen, Hermann von	15 boxes
Herzog von Braunschweig-Bevern (7 Years War)	1 box
Friedrich Wilhelm III (Napoleonic Wars)	1 box
Gneisenau, Neithart von	57 boxes
	2 folios
	2 folders
Groener, Wilhelm	28 boxes
Moltke, Helmuth von	6 boxes
	2 folios
Merts von Quirnheim, Friedrich Wilhelm	2 boxes
Roon, Albrecht von	2 boxes
Scharnhorst, Gerhard von	20 boxes
Scheuch, Heinrich	1 box
Schlieffen, Alfred von	4 boxes
Incl. Schlieffen Plan, souvenirs, personal letters,	7 folios
	1 metal box
Seeckt, Hans von	33 boxes
Winterfeldt, Hans Karl von	3 boxes

Also a collection of maps and charts and one bundle of material concerning German military cemeteries of World War I.

Contents of Miscellaneous Boxes

Misc. Box 1	1. Ms. of Ludendorff memoirs.
	2. Ms. family book of Count Lutz Schwerin von Krosigk.
	3. A folder of recommendations for military decorations.
Misc. Box 2	1. Log book of documents, 1870-71.
	2. Two log books of documents of OKH, Gruppe Rechtswesen; one of secret, one of unclassified documents
	3. One folder of important correspondence and documents Militaerverwaltung Italien, 1943-45.
Misc. Box 3	1. Papers on problems of German military government, 1940-43.
	2. Reports on Kunstpflege und Archivschutz in France, 1940-45.
	3. List of members of German military government units killed in action, 1939-44
	4. Abschlussbericht des Generalquartiermeisters ueber die deutschen Militaerverwaltungen, 1940-45. Apr. 1945.
	5. Personnel problems of German military government.
Misc. Box 4	1. Recommendations for the Kriegsverdienstkreuz, World War II,

(France under German occupation).

2. One folder of Militaerbefehlshaber Suedost. Der Chef der Militaerverwaltung; transport, finance, etc. 1942-44, mostly Yugoslav area.

3. Two bundles of photostats of church records of old German communities in Russia belonging to the collection of the Deutsche Auslands-Institut, now in the Manuscript Division of the Library of Congress.

4. An unidentified photo.

Misc. Box 5 & 6   Heeresverordnungsblaetter.
Misc. Box 7   Records of the Livonian self-government, 19th Century.
Misc. Box 8   Mobilmachung 1869.
Misc. Box 9   Mobilmachung 1870.
Misc. Box 10   Mobilmachung 1914-15.
Misc. Box 11   Mobilmachung 1915-16.
Misc. Box 12   Mobilmachung 1916-18.
Misc. Box 13   Hitler's engagement book, daily schedule in 1943. A fanciful book about the world in 50 years. Diary of Eva Braun, 1934; published in *Echo der Woche* (Munich), 1952, No. 1 and 2.

German nationalist permanent exhibit, four boxes. German military records, volumes dated 1850, 1867, 1869, 1870-71, 1882, 1883, 1884, 1885, 1903, 1912, 1913. Log book of the SS Europa.

see: U. S., Archivist of the United States (CD 3023, A3). *Thirteenth Annual Report of the Archivist of the United States*, 1946-1947, p. 67. Acc. 22'8. RG 165; Acc. 2408, RG 242.

Appendix 2

Record Group 243: Records and materials of the United States Strategic Bombing Survey for Europe.

This material is for the most part now unclassified. A comprehensive catalog of the collection exists and is now unclassified: The United States Strategic Bombing Survey, *Index to Records of the United States Strategic Bombing Survey*, June 1947, 317 pp. The collection in the National Archives is organized according to the listings in this index. The part of the collection which contains captured German documents of a non-technical nature is that of Section 64b - The Morale Division. Excerpts from the catalog listings for this part of the collection are added. There are also a few items in the records of the Military Analysis Division.

The United States Strategic Bombing Survey, *Index to Records of the United States Strategic Bombing Survey, June 1947*.

The following excerpts are of particular interest:

64b. The Effects of Strategic Bombing on German Morale (vol. I and vol. II) (final report).

j. *Mail study analysis material* (consisting of 53 envelopes). (This study was used in Vol. 2, ch. 2 of the final report.)

o. *German police activities:*

1. Gestapo arrest statistics from the cities of Bremen, Dortmund, Halle, Hamburg, Hannover, Frankfurt, Koeln, Leipzig, Muenchen, Nuernberg, Karlsruhe, Kiel, 1944.

2. Crime statistics, Hamburg, Germany, 1945.

3. Crime statistics, Bremen, Luebeck, Hamburg, Germany, 1938-1945.

4. Cases of investigation by the Bavarian police agencies, Kempten, Germany, 1942.

5. Looting; analysis of the causes of looting by persons heretofore law-abiding, survey made in Hamburg, Bremen, and Luebeck, Germany, 1944.

7. Copy of a report by the Sicherheitspolizei (security police) on occupied Holland, 28 Mar. 1945.

8. Gestapo documents giving data on the establishment and character of the intelligence system used in the cities of Halle and Merseburg and surrounding areas, March 1937.

p. *Air raid data from German cities:*

1-3. German documents giving data on Allied air raids on the cities of Strassburg, Karlsruhe, Pforzheim, Mannheim, . . . Frankfurt am Main, . . . Kassel.

4. German documents giving data on Allied air raids on the city of Cologne from 1941-45 inclusive, (consisting of 11 envelopes).

q. *General data:*

3. German documents on air raid orders, regulations and announcements, Hamburg, Germany.

6. Luftschutzbund (Association for Air Raid Protection), material on the air raid protection and relief system.

r. *German Government Data:*

1. Reichsluftfahrtministerium, Economic Section of the Plans and Intelligence Division, reports on the enemy (British-American) air war against Germany. (Berlin files).

6. A report on the morale of the people of Krefeld, Germany. Source: SS leaders and security police.

7. Reports of German officials on the conduct of the war dealing with religion.

8. Leading German officials of Germany. Reichsstimmungsberichte (morale reports) on the psychological affect of bombing on the German people.

9. German civil defense vs. aerial attack, January, 1945.

10. German and Austrian intelligence reports concerning morale on the German home front, 1944.

11. The effectiveness of propaganda in Germany as put out by the Reich Propaganda Ministry.

12. Reports of special delegates of the Ministry of Education for flak auxiliaries.

13. National Socialist German Workers Party statistics, Leipzig, Germany, March 22, 1945.

14. Material on the activities of churches and German Army chapels. Source: security police, Bielefeld, Germany.

17. Extract of German documents from the German security police files, dealing with Stimmungsberichte (morale reports) on the state of morale of the German people during the war years (consisting of four envelopes). [An S.D. card file.]

s. *Data from USSBS and other United States and British agencies:*

6. Reports on war diary and monthly statistics of the Ruestungsinspektion (Armament Inspection) Oberrhein, Germany.

t. *Miscellaneous data:*

6. Allied leaflets dropped by Anglo-American planes over Germany.

9. Captured German soldiers' diaries.

18. Labor pamphlets put out by Fritz Sauckel, Nazi labor leader, in 1943.

20. The Hitler Jugend in the war. Report No. 31, April 1944.
21. Booklets on the organization of the Gauwirtschaftskammer (county economic advisors) in Gau (county) Duesseldorf, Germany, which includes the cities of Cologne and Aachen.

Appendix 3

"Der Weltkrieg." Two hundred seventy nine vols. of the original file covered by 13 serials. Total frames 56,089.

Container	Serial No.	Bundle	Vols.	Date
1817-1822	3834 H	1- 5	1	June 1914–July 15, 1914
			2	July 16, 1914–July 21, 1914
			3- 10	July 22, 1914–July 31, 1914
			11- 24	Aug. 1, 1914–Aug. 17, 1914
1823-1828	5866 H	6- 10	25- 32	Aug. 18, 1914–Aug. 31, 1914
			33- 43	Sept. 1, 1914–Sept. 30, 1914
			44- 50	Oct. 1, 1914–Oct. 20, 1914
1881-1885	3884 H	11- 15	51- 54	Oct. 21, 1914–Oct. 31, 1914
			55- 64	Nov. 1, 1914–Nov. 30, 1914
			65- 74	Dec. 1, 1914–Dec. 31, 1914
1889-1893	3909 H	16- 20	75- 84	Jan. 1, 1915–Jan. 31, 1915
			85- 94	Feb. 1, 1915–Feb. 27, 1915
			95- 96	Feb. 28, 1915–Mar. 6, 1915
1894-1897	3930 H	21- 25	97-104	Mar. 7, 1915–Mar. 31, 1915
			105-113	Apr. 1, 1915–Apr. 30, 1915
			114-115	May 1, 1915–May 9, 1915
1898-1902	3931 H	26- 30	116-120	May 10, 1915–June 1, 1915
			121-126	June 2, 1915–June 29, 1915
			127-134	June 30, 1915–July 31, 1915
			135-136	Aug. 1, 1915–Aug. 10, 1915
1907-1912	3943 H	31- 35	137-141	Aug. 11, 1915–Aug. 30, 1915
			142-149	Aug. 31, 1915–Sept. 30, 1915
			150-157	Oct. 1, 1915–Oct. 31, 1915
1924-1928	3985 H	36- 40	158-164	Nov. 1, 1915–Nov. 28, 1915
			165-172	Nov. 29, 1915–Dec. 30, 1915
			173-178	Dec. 31, 1915–Jan. 23, 1916
1929-1933	3990 H	41- 45	179-187	Jan. 24, 1916–Feb. 29, 1916
			188-194	Mar. 1, 1916–Mar. 31, 1916
			195-197	Apr. 1, 1916–Apr. 12, 1916
1938-1949	4003 H	46- 50	198-200	Apr. 13, 1916–Apr. 27, 1916
			201-207	Apr. 28, 1916–May 31, 1916
			208-214	June 1, 1916–June 30, 1916
			215-217	July 1, 1916–July 12, 1916
1950-1952	4023 H	51- 55	218-221	July 13, 1916–July 31, 1916
			222-228	Aug. 1, 1916–Aug. 31, 1916
			229-233	Sept. 1, 1916–Sept. 28, 1916
			234-238	Sept. 29, 1916–Oct. 31, 1916
			239-240	Nov. 1, 1916–Nov. 17, 1916
1968-1975	4033 H	56- 60	241	Nov. 18, 1916–Nov. 27, 1916
			242-245	Nov. 28, 1916–Dec. 3, 1916
			246-249	Jan. 1, 1917–Jan. 31, 1917
			250-252	Feb. 1, 1917–Mar. 4, 1917
			253-255	Mar. 5, 1917–Apr. 5, 1917
			256-257	Apr. 6, 1917–Apr. 30, 1917
			258-260	May 1, 1917–May 31, 1917
			261-263	June 1, 1917–July 4, 1917

Appendix 4

"Der Weltkrieg." Secret (Geheime Akten). Thirty nine vols. of the original file covered by 21 serials. Total frames 9,217.

Container	Serial No.	Bundle	Vols.	Date
2584	5276 H	70	1	July 1914–Sept. 24, 1914
	5277 H		2	Sept. 25, 1914–Oct. 31, 1914
	5278 H		3	Nov. 1, 1914–Nov. 20, 1914
2584-2585	5279 H		4	Nov. 21, 1914–Dec. 3, 1914
2585	5280 H	71	5	Dec. 4, 1914–Dec. 31, 1914
			6	Jan. 1, 1915–Jan. 15, 1915
	5281 H		7	Jan. 16, 1915–Jan. 31, 1915
			8	Feb. 1, 1915–Feb. 10, 1915
			9	Feb. 11, 1915–Feb. 28, 1915
2585	5282 H	72	10	Mar. 1, 1915–Mar. 9, 1915
			11	Mar. 10, 1915–Mar. 20, 1915
2586-2587	5283 H		12	Mar. 21, 1915–Apr. 6, 1915
			13	Apr. 7, 1915–Apr. 20, 1915
2587	5284 H	73	14	Apr. 21, 1915–Apr. 30, 1915
			15	May 1, 1915–May 14, 1915
	5285 H		16	May 15, 1915–May 24, 1915
			17	May 25, 1915–May 31, 1915
			18	June 1, 1915–June 12, 1915
2588	5286 H	74	19	June 13, 1915–July 9, 1915
			20	July 10, 1915–Aug. 2, 1915
2589	5287 H		21	Aug. 3, 1915–Aug. 25, 1915
			22	Aug. 26, 1915–Sept. 21, 1915
2590	5288 H	75	23	Sept. 22, 1915–Oct. 8, 1915
			24	Oct. 9, 1915–Nov. 8, 1915
	5289 H		25	Nov. 9, 1915–Dec. 7, 1915

2591	5290 H	76	26	Dec. 8, 1915–Dec. 31, 1915
2592	5291 H		27	Jan. 1, 1916–Feb. 29, 1916
			28	Mar. 1, 1916–Mar. 11, 1916
2593	5292 H		28a	Mar. 12, 1916–Apr. 15, 1916
			29	Apr. 16, 1916–May 31, 1916
2594	5293 H	77	30	June 1, 1916–July 14, 1916
			31	July 15, 1916–July 27, 1916
			32	July 28, 1916–Aug. 31, 1916
2595	5294 H		33	Sept. 1, 1916–Oct. 5, 1916
		78	34	Oct. 6, 1916–Nov. 8, 1916
			35	Nov. 9, 1916–Dec. 31, 1916
2596	5295 H		36	Jan. 1, 1917–Feb. 27, 1917
			37	Feb. 28, 1917–May 31, 1917
2597	5296 H	79	38	June 1, 1917–Aug. 15, 1917
			39	Aug. 16, 1917–Dec. 31, 1917

Appendix 5

"Peace moves of the Central Powers" (Die Friedensaktion der Zentralmaechte). Eighteen vols. of original files. One serial in nine containers. Total frames 3,773.

Container	Serial No.	Bundle	Vols.	Date
2000-2008	4058 H	467-470	1- 6	Oct. 18, 1916–Dec. 31, 1916
			7- 13	Jan. 1, 1917–May 31, 1918
			14- 18	June 1, 1918–Oct. 1, 1918

Appendix 6

"Mediation," "Peace moves and tendencies." Sixty seven vols. of original files covered by four serials. Total frames 15,364.
a) Vols. 1-27: Mediation (Vermittlungsaktion).

Container	Serial No.	Bundle	Vols.	Date
2073 2080	4126 H	114-117	1- 3	Aug. 8, 1914–Jan. 31, 1915
			4- 10	Feb. 1, 1915–Jan. 18, 1916
			11- 13	Jan. 19, 1916–May 7, 1916
2081-2088	4149 H	117-121	14- 23	May 8, 1916–Dec. 31, 1916
			24- 27	Jan. 1, 1917–Feb. 23, 1917

b) Vols. 28-67: Peace moves and tendencies (Friedensstimmungen und Aktionen zur Vermittlung des Friedens).

Container	Serial No.	Bundle	Vols.	Date
2089-2098	4194 H	122-126	28- 32	Feb. 24, 1917–Apr. 30, 1917
			33- 44	May 1, 1917–Sept. 13, 1917
2099-2103	4213 H	127-132	45- 55	Sept. 14, 1917–Nov. 25, 1917
			56- 62	Nov. 26, 1917–Dec. 26, 1917
			63- 67	Dec. 27, 1917–Feb. 6, 1918

Appendix 7

"Mediation," "Peace moves and tendencies." Secret (Geheime Akten). Fifty four vols. of the original file covered by three serials. Total frames 14,487.
a) Vols. 1-30: Mediation.

Container	Serial No.	Bundle	Vols.	Date
2104-2115	4272 H	139-143	1	Dec. 9, 1914–Dec. 31, 1914
			2- 6	Jan. 1, 1915–Apr. 30, 1915
			7- 14	May 1, 1915–Dec. 31, 1915
			15- 19	Jan. 1, 1916–July 11, 1916
2116-2128	4301 H	144-148	20- 27	July 12, 1916–Dec. 31, 1916
			28- 30	Jan. 1, 1917–Mar. 30, 1917

b) Vols. 31-54: Peace moves and tendencies.

Container	Serial No.	Bundle	Vols.	Date
2160-2170	4326 H	149-152	31- 36	Mar. 31, 1917–May 16, 1917
			37- 43	May 17, 1917–June 30, 1917
			44- 49	July 1, 1917–Sept. 30, 1917
			50- 54	Oct. 1, 1917–Dec. 25, 1917

Appendix 8

Outbreak of war.

Container	Serial No.	Bundle	Vols.	Date
2073	4126 H	105	1	June 28, 1914–July 21, 1914

Appendix 9

U.S.A. August 1917 - October 1918.

3021	6593	553	3- 4	

NETHERLANDS STATE INSTITUTE
FOR WAR-DOCUMENTATION
AMSTERDAM

GERMAN documents in the custody of the Netherlands State Institute for War-Documentation are grouped according to the headings given below. These documents were at the Institute in 1950. The information given below is taken from Netherlands, Ministrie van Onderwijs, Kunsten en Wetenschappen, *Jaarverslag 1950, Rijksinstituut voor Oorlogsdocumentatie* ('S-Gravenhage, 1951), pp. 25-26, where more details concerning the holdings, organization, and publication plans of the Institute can be found.

Reichskommissar fuer die besetzten niederlaendischen Gebiete:

Praesidialabteilung (No. 27); six linear meters, organized, indexed.

Oberkasse (No. 27a); eight m, provisionally organized.
Notstandsbeihilfe des Reichskommissars (No. 28); one m, provisionally organized.
Generalkommissar fuer Verwaltung und Justiz (No. 29); 80 m, organized, two-thirds indexed.

Gnadenabteilung (No. 29a); four m, organized, unindexed.

Generalstrafanwaltschaft (Strafdossiers) (No. 29b); 18 m, provisionally organized.

Generalkommissar fuer Finanz und Wirtschaft (Ernaehrung und Landwirtschaft, Forst-und Holzwirtschaft, Preisbildung, Bauwesen, Ein- und Ausfuhr, Kartellreferat, Wirtschaftspruefstelle) (No. 20); 60 m. provisionally organized, party indexed.

Generalkommissar zur besonderen Verwendung (No. 31); nine m, organized, partly indexed.

Hauptabteilung Soziale Verwaltung (No. 32); one m, organized, partly indexed.

Hauptabteilung Gewerbliche Wirtschaft (Ruestungsinspektion) (No. 33); 50 m, organized.

Beauftragter des Reichskommissars fuer die Provinz Zeeland (No. 34); four m, organized.

Beauftragter des Reichskommissars fuer die Provinz Limburg (No. 35); three m, provisionally organized.

Vormundschaftsgericht (No. 36); two m, organized.

Amtliche deutsche Beratungsstellen (No. 37); one m, provisionally organized.

Hoeherer SS- und Polizeifuehrer Niederlande (No. 38); organized, unindexed.

Befehlshaber der Sicherheitspolizei und des Sicherheitsdienstes (No. 38a); one m, organized.

Befehlshaber der Ordnungspolizei No. 38b); two m, organized.

Ein- und Ausreisestelle Maastricht (No. 38c); 40 m, partly organized.

Zentralstelle fuer juedische Auswanderung (No. 38d); two and one-half m, unorganized, unindexed.

Durchgangslager Westerbork (No. 38e); 12 m, organized.

Concentration Camp Vught (No. 39); 20 m, organized.

Other concentration camps (No. 40); 15 m, organized.

Deutsche Wehrmacht (No. 41); six m, organized, indexed.

Organisation Todt (No. 42); one m, provisionally organized.

Technische Nothilfe (No. 43); one m, provisionally organized.

Zentralauftragstelle (No. 44); five m, unorganized, unindexed.

Arbeitsbereich der NSDAP in den Niederlanden (No. 45); 20 m, provisionally organized, unindexed.

Hilfsausschuss fuer die Deutschen in den Niederlanden (No. 46); three m, provisionally organized.

NOTE: According to the publication cited above, closely related document groups are deposited in the Algemeen Rijksarchief (General State Archives). Among these are records of the Wehrmachtbefehlshaber in den Niederlanden.

Chapter 6

YIDDISH SCIENTIFIC INSTITUTE—YIVO (NEW YORK)

I. *Hauptamt Wissenschaft.* (G 293-298.) Amt Wissenschaftsbeobachtung und -Wertung in the office of Alfred Rosenberg as "Beauftragter des Fuehrers fuer die Ueberwachung der gesamten geistigen und weltanschaulichen Schulung der NSDAP."

This collection, the only complete one in the YIVO, is separated from the main collection (Ministry of Propaganda.) It has not been cataloged at all. It consists of about 12 folders, each containing about 300 pages. The folders and documents are in alphabetical order according to names of academic personnel, teachers, researchers, writers, etc.

Three separate folders contain documents pertaining to particular universities, scientific institutions, and academic conferences. The file containing the documents beginning with letter "A" is missing at the time of this report.

While most of the file in the alphabetical folders of the HAW consists of correspondence up to 20 pages, two files are outstanding by their mere quantity of pages, several hundred each, and by the degree of actual research that has gone into the preparation of the two files. The first is on the poet *Stefan George* and his circle, the second on *Ludwig Klages* and his followers.

II. *The collection of documents of the Reich Ministry for Propaganda*

The collection of captured German documents in YIVO, besides the special collection "Hauptamt Wissenschaft", consists of about 70 folders. It has been cataloged by a member of the Institute.

The documents seem to stem mainly from the archives of the German Ministerium fuer Volksaufklaerung und Propaganda, the Goebbels Ministry. None of the special collections is complete. On some territories of eastern Europe, e. g., the Baltic States, more material is to be found than on Hungary or Bulgaria.

III. A volume, formerly the property of Kurt Daluege, entitled "Fire in the Reichstag Building, a collection of photographs." It contains eight different photographs of the "Guilty Man," van der Lubbe, 21 pictures of the halls in the Reichstag Building, showing damage and destruction due to the fire, four views of the hall where plenary sessions were held, and a series of other photographs, chiefly of objects found on van der Lubbe's person.

IV. A Reichssicherheitshauptamt (RSHA) file, concerning the assassination of the Deputy Reich Governor Reinhard Heydrich in Prague. This contains two volumes, with four sketches and 49 photographs showing a reconstruction of the crime, objects found, as well as photographs of the criminals and their alleged accomplices. In addition, there is a final report with six supplementary files on the activities of parachutists trained in England and on the measures taken to elucidate the crime. These concern short-wave messages by the parachutists, administrative and penal measures, use of the regular police, and reprisals against the town of Lidice. The file also contains verdicts of the military courts in Prague and Brno, also reports on the reaction of the Czech radio in London and the effect of these measures on the Czech population.

V. Eighty-two files containing newspaper clippings about Goebbels that appeared between 1921 and 1943. The files were kept by Goebbels himself and arranged according to periods and events.

VI. Documents relating to the withdrawal of citizenship from certain German subjects.

VII. Three secret, mimeographed, memoranda from the Statistische Reichsamt:
1. Die Entwicklung der Kriminalitaet im Deutschen Reich vom Kriegsbeginn bis Mitte 1943.
2. Kriminalitaet im Grossdeutschen Reich im Jahr 1942.
3. Jugendkriminalitaet im Grossdeutschen Reich im Jahr 1942 und im 1. Halbjahr 1943.

(German criminality statistics have been published in *Wirtschaft und Statistik* only up to June 30, 1940.)

VIII. Reichsministerium des Innern, Der Sachverstaendige fuer Rassenforschung (Expert for Racial Research, Reich Ministry of the Interior). One thousand seven hundred-forty genealogical reports which mostly concern the descendants of the inter-related families of Mendelssohn and Itzig (Hitzig), and were probably collected with a view to bringing the family tree of the Mendelssohns up to date.

(NOTE: Items III-VI and VIII are excerpted from an article by Bruno Blau, in *Wiener Library Bulletin*, Vol. V (1951), No. 1-2, pp. 9).

PART IV

Special Supplement

PUBLICATIONS OF DOCUMENTS CAPTURED BY THE GERMANS

INFORMATION ON DOCUMENTS CAPTURED BY THE GERMANS
BEFORE OR DURING WORLD WAR II.

Germany, Auswaertiges Amt. *Polnische Dokumente zur Vorgeschichte des Krieges.* Berlin: Deutscher Verlag, 1940. Weissbuch 3. Captured Polish documents. Facsimiles. (D735.G3 7512)

Germany, Auswaertiges Amt. *Dokumente zur englisch-franzoesischen Politik der Kriegsausweitung.* Berlin: Buch-und Tiefdruck Gesellschaft m.b.H., 1940. Weissbuch 4. Captured English, French, and Norwegian documents. Facsimiles. (D735.G45)

Germany, Auswaertiges Amt. *Weitere Dokumente zur Kriegsausweitungspolitik der Westmaechte. Die Generalstabsbesprechungen Englands und Frankreichs mit Belgien und den Niederlanden.* Berlin: Zentralverlag der NSDAP, Franz Eher Verlag Nachf, G.m.b.H., 1940. Weissbuch 5. Captured English, French, Belgian and Dutch documents. Facsimiles. (D735.G46, 1940)

Germany, Auswaertiges Amt. France, Armée, Etat-major. *Die Geheimakten des franzoesischen Generalstabs.* Berlin: Zentralverlag der NSDAP, Franz Eher Nachf. G.m.b.H., 1941. Weissbuch 6. Captured French documents, includes facsimiles of all. (D761.A4, 1941g)

Germany, Auswaertiges Amt. *Dokumente zum Konflikt mit Jugoslawien und Griechenland.* Berlin: Deutscher Verlag, 1941. Weissbuch 7. Captured French documents mainly. A Polish document is included. (D733.G726, 1941)

Berber, Friedrich, (ed.). *Deutschland-England 1933-1939, Die Dokumente des deutschen Friedenswillens.* Essen: Essener Verlagsanstalt, 1940. Contains a few Czech documents.

Berber, Friedrich (ed.). *Europaeische Politik, 1933-1938, im Spiegel der Prager Akten.* 3rd. ed. Essen: Essener Verlagsanstalt, 1942. Captured Czech documents, mostly excerpts. (D455.B46, 1941)

Deutsche Informationsstelle. *Dokumente britisch-franzoesischer Grausamkeit, Die britische und franzoesische Kriegsfuehrung in den Niederlanden, Belgien und Nordfrankreich im Mai 1940.* Berlin: Volk und Reich Verlag, 1940. Contains several captured French Army documents; most of the non-German material is dated *after* the German occupation of the various areas. (D804.G7D4)

Germany, Auswaertiges Amt. *Bolschewistische Verbrechen gegen Kriegsrecht und Menschlichkeit.* Berlin: Deutscher Verlag, 1941-
1. Folge (1941). Contains one captured Russian Army document; pp. 804-5.
2. Folge (1942). Contains several captured Russian Army documents.
3. Folge (1943). Contains several captured Russian Army documents. (D804.R964.)

Germany, Auswaertiges Amt. *Dokumente ueber die Alleinschuld Englands am Bombenkrieg gegen die Zivilbevoelkerung.* Berlin: Deutscher Verlag, 1943. Weissbuch Nr. 8, contains captured French, Dutch, Polish, and Yugoslav documents. (JX5142.G42, 1943.)

Germany, Auswaertiges Amt. *Voelkerrechtliche Dokumente ueber Afrika.* Band I. 1880-1918. Berlin: Reichsdruckerei, 1942. "Nur fuer den Dienstgebrauch." Certain of the documents in this collection appear to be hitherto unpublished documents captured by the Germans in the French and Belgian archives. (DT1.G45.)

Germany, Auswaertiges Amt. *Voelkerrechtsverletzungen der britischen Streitkraefte und der Zivilbevoelkerung auf Kreta.* Berlin: Deutscher Verlag, 1942, contains captured British consular papers. (D766.3, G4, 1942.)

Germany, Auswaertiges Amt. Archivkommission; France, Ambassade, Russia. *Un Diplomate Français Parle du Péril Bolcheviste, Rapports de Jean Herbette, Ambassadeur de France à Moscou (1927-1931).* [Berlin?]: Imprimerie de Sceaux, 1943. Full texts in French and a few facsimiles. (DK270.F7, 1943.)

See also "Tschechen-Dokumente beweisen Englands Kriegswillen," in *Voelkischer Beobachter* (Berliner Ausgabe), 10 December 1939, pp. 1-2. Five Czech Documents; reports of the Czech Embassy in London, 1938.

Captured documents published by the Germans in the *Monatshefte fuer Auswaertige Politik:* (JX.5A8)

Vol. VII (1940), 5-13.
Werner Frauendienst, "Ein ungehoerter Warner." Memoranda and letters of the pro-German Polish Professor Studnicki to Polish

69

Foreign Minister Beck, 1939. Text and commentary.

Vol. VII (1940), 104-5.

"Ein tschechisches Geheimdokument ueber die franzoesische Aussenpolitik." Parts of a commentary on a report of Czech Ambassador to Paris Osusky of 25 Nov. 1933.

Vol. IX (1942), 655-60.

Friedrich Berber, "Zur Englischen Vorkriegsgeschichte." Three memoranda from the Czech archives reporting on talks with British statesmen, 1938.

Vol. X (1943), 429-38.

Hans Uebersberger, "Das entscheidende Aktenstueck zur Kriegsschuldfrage, 1914." Document, presumably captured in the Yugoslav archives, allegedly indicates that Dimitrijević, head of the Black Hand, was encouraged by the Russian Military Attaché in Belgrade, Colonel Artamonov, to organize the plot to assassinate the Archduke Francis Ferdinand of Austria and that Russia would back Serbia in case of a conflict with Austria (all this is not in the document).

Vol. X (1943), 658-70.

"Das wahre Gesicht des Bolschewismus. Geheimberichte des tschechischen Gesandten in Moskau und des tschechischen Generalkonsuls in Kiew aus den Jahren 1931-37." The text of a number of Czech documents, one from 1936, one from 1938, and the rest from

1936 and 1937, some in full, some excerpted.

The following are titles of articles which appeared in the *Leipziger Neueste Nachrichten* and which probably contained reprints of documents captured by the Germans. The newspaper is not available in the United States for the years listed.

"Sensationelle polnische Geheimdokumente," March 31, 1940.

"Polendokumente klaeren," April 2, 1940.

"In Oslo gefundene Dokumente des Norwegischen Aussenministeriums," May 3, 1940.

"Koenig Leopold von Belgien stellt England und Frankreich an den Pranger," (Denkschrift) June 8, 1940.

"Dokumente nageln die Schuld der Westmaechte fest," June 29, 1940.

"Geheimakten Gamelins erbeutet," July 4, 5, 6, 7, 9, 11, 15, 16, and 24, 1940.

"Zwei Dokumente aus den in La Charité erbeuteten Geheimakten des franzoesischen Generalstabs," January 1, 1941.

"Entlarvung der Friedensstoerer auf dem Balkan," (144 Dokumente) June 19, 1941.

"Erbeuteter Geheimbefehl Stalins," August 10, 1942.

"Neues Dokument fuer die gegnerische Kriegsschuld," (Dok. Nr. 1783 W.O.B. London, Dec. 18, 1920), Nov. 28, 1943.

Addenda

71

THE FOLLOWING information was received after the main body of the manuscript had been prepared for the printer. The material here is, however, covered by the index.

Books

Best, S. Payne. *The Venlo Incident*. London: Hutchinson and Co. Ltd., 1950. Facing pp. 208 and 209 is a reproduction of an order of Reichssicherheitshauptamt (RSHA) Amt IV of April 5, 1945, concerning certain important prisoners, like Franz Halder and Kurt von Schuschnigg, and ordering the execution of Georg Elser of the Buergerbraeu bomb plot. (D805.G3B477.)

Germany, Auswaertiges Amt. "Documents concerning the Swedish Newspaper *Dagens Nyheter*." Stockholm: Ministry of Foreign Affairs, 1952. Press release of the Swedish Foreign Ministry on January 24, 1952, concerning the newspaper *Dagens Nyheter*. Contains excerpt from one and full text of two documents between February and November 1940 from the German Foreign Ministry Archives.

Halder, Franz. *The Halder Diaries*. 7 vols. (mimeographed). Washington: Infantry Journal Press, 1950. Translation of the text of the diary of Franz Halder, former Chef des Generalstabs des Heeres im Oberkommando des Heeres (OKH), for the period 14 August 1939-24 September 1942. (DD247.H25A8,1950.)

Nikitin, M.N., and Vagin, P.I. *The Crimes of the German Fascists in the Leningrad Region*. London: Hutchinson and Co. Ltd., 1946. Quotes a number of German documents, mostly relating to local affairs, from the northern section of the German occupied areas of the U.S.S.R. (see especially pp. 55-68). (D804.G4N52.)

Netherlands, Staten General, Tweede Kamer, Enquêtecommisie Regeringsbeleid 1940-1945. *Ministers — en Kabinetcrises, Voorbereiding Terugkeer, Bijlagen* (5B) 'S-Gravenhage: Staatsdrukkerij-en Uitgeverijbedrijf, 1950. See pp. 557-62 for documents, mostly by the Reichskommissar fuer die besetzten niederlaendischen Gebiete, Beauftragter des Reichkommissars fuer die Provinz Suedholland, concerning negotiations of the Reichskommissar with the Allies, April, 1945. (DJ287.A53.)

Wilmot, Chester. *The Struggle for Europe*. New York: Harper and Brothers, Publishers, 1952. See pp. 719-25 for "A Note on Sources." The unpublished sources used are mainly from the German Army, the German Navy, and the Reichsministerium fuer Ruestung und Kriegsproduktion. (D743.W53,1952.)

Periodicals

Aufbau (DS101.A75)

(New World Club, New York)

Vol. 12 (1946), No. 28, p. 7.
Alfred Rosenberg to Joseph Goebbels, 2 July 1942 (on the 80th birthday of Gerhart Hauptmann).

Vol. 13 (1947), No. 23, p. 3.
An article quotes the *Mittelbayerische Zeitung*, Regensburg, to the effect that Adolf Hitler's membership card in the Deutsche Arbeiterpartei, signed by Anton Drexler on 1 January 1920, was No. 555, not No. 7, as publicly announced.

Vol. 13 (1947), No. 24, p. 3.
Schwerin-Krosigk to Goebbels, 6 April 1945; [Schwerin-Krosigk (?)] to Goebbels, 14 April 1945.

Vol. 13 (1947), No. 41, p. 3.
Aufzeichnung betreff. Zentrales Judenamt in Paris; Besprechung Abetz, Danneker, Achenbach, Zeitschel, 28 February 1941. From the files of the Deutsche Botschaft Paris now at the Centre de Documentation Juive Contemporaine (see also Vol. 13, No. 46, p. 3).

Vol. 14 (1948), No. 28, p. 1.
A document from the Reichssicherheitshauptamt: Kaltenbrunner to the Grand Mufti Amin el Husseini, 29 October 1943.

Vol. 16 (1950), No. 24, pp. 1-2; No. 25, pp. 7-8; No. 26, pp. 5-6.
Kempner, Robert M.W., "Der Mann, der den Weltkrieg verhindern wollte." The kidnapping of Berthold Jacob. Documents from the German Foreign Ministry, dated 1934-1935.

United Nations World (JX1901.U54)

Vol. 4 (1950), No. 3, pp. 7-9.
Kempner, Robert M. W. "Stalin's 'Separate Peace in 1943." This article refers to several memoranda by Reichsaussenminister Ribbentrop, dated 1942-44, concerning a separate peace with the Soviet Union.

Zeitschrift fuer die gesamte Strafrechtswissenschaft (Berlin).

Vol 84 (1952), No. 1, pp. 81-81.
Blau, Bruno, "Die Kriminalitaet in Deutschland waehrend des zweiten Weltkriegs." An article based on secret memoranda of the Statistische Reichsamt in YIVO; see Part III, Chapter 6, item VII.

Depositories

Library of Congress, Manuscripts Division, Appendix 2, continued.
The German Submarine Materials. Ac. D. R. F-1850, 2366
(NOTE: The following is the continuation of the list to be found on p. 50).

Box	Contents	Date
14	Material concerning "U-977."	1941-45
	Material concerning "U-1064."	
	Papers of Otto Bickenbach.	1933-43
15	Analysis of raw products.	1941-44
	Two volumes in English concerning lighthouses.	1831 and 1833
	Chemical manual.	1941
	A manual concerning the nomenclature and operation of M[achine] G[un] 17.	
	Two volumes concerning weather.	1936-37
16	File of correspondence on coastal alarm units (Infantry); including organization, signal, pass-words, precautions against paratroop landings.	1944-45
	Folder from Marineleitung prepared for Unterseeboots-Abwehrschule.	1934
	Reports of the Rumanian General Staff on the mining of the Danube.	1943
	Index of restricted and unrestricted books.	
	Directions for the operations of a hand lubrication pump.	
	Orders, forms, logs, and reports.	
	Notebook of Otto Fricke and companion book for aneroid barometer; in one folder.	
17	Log books, work book and assorted notebooks concerning German submarines and submarine schools. All are stamped "Armada Argentina División Submarinos."	ca. 1944
18	Miscellaneous submarine material — log books, notebooks, etc.	1943-45
19	An die Deutsche Gesandtschaft, Hsinking (Manchukuo).	1944
	Gefechtskizze.	
	Village statistics, Saida.	1941
	Letter to Frau Anita Mohr, Tokyo, from Else Sandkuhl, Berlin, Oct. 1, 1943. Weltkarte (with ship routes).	
	Miscellaneous material concerning machinery and patents	1940, 1944-1945
	Notebook concerning American ships entitled "Naval vessels status."	ca. 1920
	Folder of personal letters, photographs and drawings.	1944
	Package of material, in Japanese, concerning agriculture, food supply and consumption, etc. in Europe.	ca. 1941
20	Material concerning goods scheduled to be dispatched on returning blockade runners.	
	Miscellaneous material concerning submarines.	
	Miscellaneous material.	ca. 1944

Library of Congress, Prints and Photographs Division.

Lot Nos. 5680-700. Deutscher Lichbild-Dienst G.m.b.H. (Deutscher Bildspielbund e.V.), Auslandsabteilung. One thousand six hundred and twenty cards, each with a small, clear, photograph and an informative caption, apparently designed for use by a commentator when the corresponding lantern slide was shown. Subjects: architecture in Germany, Hitler Youth activities, housing projects, folk art, etc.

Additional Books

Fischer, George. *Soviet Opposition to Stalin.* Cambridge: Harvard University Press, 1952. Cites some German documents from the Hoover Institute and the Yiddish Scientific Institute.

Germany, Auswaertiges Amt. *Akten zur deutschen auswaertigen Politik, 1918-45,* Serie D.
III. *Deutschland und der spanische Buergerkrieg, 1936-39* (1952).
IV. *Die Nachwirkungen von Muenchen, Oktober 1938—Maerz 1939* (1952). (see pp. 3-4).

Germany, Office of Military Government for Bavaria, Economics Division. "Post-War Status of Archives, Libraries, Museums in Land Bayern," with two supplements. 1946. Pp. 48 (mimeographed). Detailed information on the pre-war holdings and present status of archives, libraries, and museums in Bavaria; organized alphabetically by city. (National Archives Call No. CD1810.G4,1946).

Germany, Office of Military Government for Bavaria, Monuments, Fine Arts and Archives Section. "Post-War Status of Chief Archival Institutions in Bavaria (as of 1 January 1948)," 1948. Pp. 37 (mimeographed). Detailed information on the pre-war holdings, war-time fate, and present status of archives in Bavaria, organized alphabetically by city. (National Archives Call No. CD1810.G4,1948).

International Refugee Organization. *Claim of the International Refugee Organization to Diamonds Looted by Nazis and Recovered by the U. S. Military Authorities in Germany.* 1 July 1949. See Appendix III for the text of a document of Der Militaerbefehlshaber Belgien und Nordfrankreich, Militaerverwaltungschef, 7 May 1942, concerning diamonds confiscated by the Germans. English translation, pp. 20-21. (HV640.8.I6)

McDonald, Charles B., and Mathews, Sidney T. *The European Theater of Operations,*

Three Battles: Arnaville, Altuzzo, and Schmidt. (United States Army in World War II). United States, Department of the Army, Historical Division. Washington: Government Printing Office, 1952. The volume is divided into three parts: "River Crossing at Arnaville," "Breakthrough at Monte Altuzzo," and "Objective: Schmidt." German military records are cited in the footnotes. See the bibliographical notes on pp. 99, 245, and 421.

Stacey, C. P. *The Canadian Army*, 1939-1945. Ottawa: Edmund Cloutier, 1948. Published by authority of the Minister of National Defense. This book cites German military documents pertaining to the Dieppe, Sicilian, Italian, and Normandy campaigns. (D768.15.A45)

Szternfinkiel, Natan Eliasz. *Zaglada Zydów Sosnowca* [The Extermination of the Jews of Sosnowiec (Sosnowitz)]. Katowice: Centralna Zydowska Komisja Historyczna [Central Jewish Historical Commission], 1946. German text of 14 documents from German police archives in Upper Silesia. Originals in the Archives of the Central Jewish Historical Commission in Poland. (D765.2.S689)

Other Additional Material

Supplement to Part I, Appendix 2, p. 7

DENMARK

Denmark, Rigsdagen, Folketinget, Kommission af 25. Oktober 1950 i henhold til Grundlovens #45. *Beretning til Folketinget*, Vol. XII, *Tyske Dokumenter*. København: J. H. Schultz, 1951. This report is based on a collection of captured German documents which are reprinted in German and Danish in a supplementary volume (Bilag). The sources of the documents are given in the *Bilag*, pp. xi-xii. Included are items from the Oberkommando der Wehrmacht (OKW), Hoeheres Kommando z.b.V. XXXI, Gruppe XXI, and other military organizations; and documents from the files of the German Foreign Ministry.

NOTE: A number of the documents published in this volume and in other Scandinavian publications of German documents have been reprinted in Walther Hubatsch, *Die deutsche Besetzung von Daenemark und Norwegen*, 1940, Goettinger Beitraege fuer Gegenwartsfragen, No. 5 (Goettingen, 1952), pp. 407-473.

Die Welt als Geschichte (Supplement to Part II, p. 18)

Vol. 12 (1952), 61-68.

Bernhard Poll, "Vom Schicksal der deutschen Heeresakten und der amtlichen Kriegsgeschichtsschreibung." See pp. 65-68 on the fate of German military records during and at the end of World War II.

Hoover Institute and Library

Nationalsozialistischer Dozentenbund (supplement to Part III, Chapter 2, Item 3, p. 25). This file consists of letters from the Reichsamtsleiter, NS Dozentenbund, Munich, containing information on candidates applying for grants from the Deutsche Forschungsgemeinschaft (Notgemeinschaft der Deutschen Wissenschaft). The file is alphabetized according to the applicants' names.

Supplement to Part IV, p. 69

Reinoehl, Fritz von (ed.). *Grossserbische Umtriebe vor und nach Ausbruch des ersten Weltkrieges.* Germany, Reichsarchiv Wien. *Veroeffentlichungen*, Reihe 1, Vol. I. *Der Fall Jeftanović-Sola-Gavrila.* Wien: A. Holzhausens Nachf., 1944. Documents captured by the Germans in Yugoslavia from the Archiv der bosnisch-herzegowinischen Landesregierung, Archiv der Bezirkshauptmannschaft Ragusa, and the Registratur der bosnisch-herzegowinischen Abteilung des k.u.k. Gemeinsamen Finanzministeriums. (DR 340.R45. Rare Bk. Coll.)

Supplement to "The German Submarine Materials," 'U-977' p. 74

Schaeffer, Heinz. *U-Boat* 977. London: W. Kimber, 1952. It has not been possible to examine a copy of this book. (D782.U2S34,1952)

Deutsche Rundschau (continued from Part II, p. 16)

Vol. 78 (1952), "Aus den Seeckt-Dokumenten:"

pp. 881-91. "Die Verabschiedung Seeckts 1926."

pp. 1013-23. "Seeckt und die Innenpolitik."

Library of Congress, Microfilm Section

(Part III, Chapter 3, Section V, p. 31)

Germany, Reichsarchiv. *Der Weltkrieg*, 1914 bis 1918. Vol. XIV. *Kriegfuehrung im Winter 1917-18. Der Wendepunkt der Kriegslage. Das Waffenstillstandsersuchen.* Berlin: E. S. Mittler & Sohn, 1943. This volume has not yet been published. The Library of Congress has a microfilm copy (positive) made from the corrected page proof by the German War Documents Project. (Microfilm D-18)

INDEX

FOR THE USE of the index the following points should be kept in mind: The nature of the material covered by the *Guide* makes exhaustive subject indexing impossible. Thus, for instance, the Reheo-Archiv is a general source on many aspects of German and Nazi Party History, the Auswaertiges Amt for German foreign relations, and the Himmler Files for the organization and wide range of activities of the SS. It is essential that researchers interested in specific subjects look not only under the subject headings, but also under the names of those agencies whose files may contain relevant information.

Geographical terms are used in their English version. For German government and party agencies the official German title is used, regardless of the form to be found in the text. All German government agencies are listed alphabetically, while those of the Nazi Party are grouped under the Party's German name. Under the heading "Germany," a detailed listing of German governmental, political, industrial, and private organizations has been compiled in order to provide a general survey of most of the material covered by the index.

The index is largely the work of Roger W. Nelson and Ralph Mavrogordato.

INDEX

84

INDEX

DEPARTMENT OF THE AIR FORCE
Muir S. Fairchild Research Information Center (AETC)
600 Chennault Circle
Maxwell Air Force Base, Alabama 36112-6010

19 March 2008

MEMORANDUM FOR DTIC
ATTN: DTIC-OQ

FROM: AUL/ES

SUBJECT: Document AD074148

Please change the distribution statement for the above DTIC report from Limited to US Government and US Government Contractors to Approved for Public Release; Distribution is Unlimited.

I. V. GENE JOHNSON
Security Manager

www.ingramcontent.com/pod-product-compliance
Lightning Source LLC
Chambersburg PA
CBHW081340090426

42737CB00017B/3221